7 Costly Mistakes When Choosing a Publisher

Self-Publishing Secrets
That Will Save You Thousands

By Melanie Johnson & Jenn Foster

Melanie Johnson & Jenn Foster

Elite Online Publishing
63 East 11400 South Suite #230
Sandy, UT 84070

www.EliteOnlinePublishing.com

ISBN: 978-1-956642-46-9 (eBook)
ISBN: 978-1-956642-45-2 (Paperback)

DEDICATION

To everyone who has ever thought about writing a book.

YOU can write a book.

YOU can be an author.

Share your story.

Leave a legacy.

To get help publishing or marketing your book visit
EliteOnlinePublishing.com
There you can find current publishing and marketing
tools, tips and secrets.

TABLE OF CONTENTS

ACKNOWLEDGEMENTS

First and foremost we are so grateful to God for blessing us, our families and our business and making all this possible. Our Kids, Nathan & Justice, for always pushing me and encouraging to do more and be better and keeping me on my toes !! I'm thankful every day that you are my sons.

I'm grateful for Bailey, Carson & Brendan, for your patience and support. You help me understand the meaning of life! I feel so blessed to have a cheerleader for a mom. Thanks, Mom for always being there for me.

To our families, for all the support, love and standing by us through thick and thin.

1. Chasing Your Self-Publishing Dream

If you are thinking of joining countless numbers of people, who are considering self-publishing their book, now is the right time to read this book. There are several reasons why you should consider this option. The publishing world has come a long way in the last century. It is witnessing some of the most dynamic changes in the recent past. There was a time when traditional printing was the de facto standard for the publishing world. However, the trend is slowly shifting of late, especially in the last two decades. With the use of the internet and virtual technology, traditional publishing is experiencing a phase of churning and upheaval. Many traditional publishers have closed down their operations either fully or partially, and they are entering the exciting world of self and e-publishing. Amazon has already surpassed Barnes and Noble as the largest book retailer in the world, while other medium to smaller players are already facing the immense heat of global competition, especially from the self-publishing world.

E-book publishing is a multi-billion dollar industry. It is exploding every day too. More numbers of authors are trying hard to get their books published and released through self-publishing. Traditional publishers are very difficult to approach because they have their share of barriers, corporate rules, and regulations. In fact, the total numbers of traditional books are decreasing every year. For those writers who eventually get a traditional book contract, a depressing reality starts creeping in as the time progresses; all traditional publishers have either tight marketing budgets or too little time for new authors. In other words, new authors may have to spend their own money to market and promote their books. Above all, royalty rate fixed for a published book is very low and often minuscule. On top of that, they lose control and ownership of their book and It could take over 2 years to get it to the marketplace.

If you are serious about publishing your book, self-publishing is a great decision and the effort is well worth it. If you have a great self-publishing company behind you, your book and your business will be even more successful than with a traditional publisher. The growth in book publishing is the most visible in self-publishing because the industry is witnessing an enormous growth in the number of titles produced in the self-published category. Although the self-publishing market is more packed than ever before, your chances of publishing a book are as bright and promising as anyone else who is also trying to publish. The rapid advent of internet technology is a great enabler! In fact, it offers an equal book publishing opportunity to all. A majority of readers are buying e-reading devices to read their books. ebook publishing, along with print on demand (POD), will be the standard for publishing and it will remain so for years in the future.

However, there are many caveats here that you may need to evaluate and examine. It is true that publishing is becoming easier day-by-day. However, succeeding in a competitive minefield is never easy. To be successful, you will need to create a product that fills the vacuum that exists today. In other words, you will have to produce a niche market for your book. In addition, you will also need a solid marketing plan that can launch your online presence. Nonetheless, succeeding in self-publishing is far more rewarding than the experience that you get while trying to publish your book in a traditional way. This book is for those aspiring writers, who are interested in self-publishing. It is more likely that a number of authors have had the terrible experience of dealing with traditional publishers. Most likely, the frustration of getting rejection letters from them is too agonizing. Those authors who were successful in landing traditional contracts may have ceded more than their expectations. In fact, a traditional publisher eventually emerges as a clear winner by placing questionable demands and unjustified requests.

This book discusses typical problems that a writer faces while negotiating a book contract deal with a traditional publisher. A majority of publishers demand full book rights from the author during the contract signing process. Lack of proper marketing and promotion, non-cooperation in establishing an author-centered web presence and charging excessive upfront costs are some other critical issues that an author should consider. Apart from these traditional publisher related issues, new authors may also commit countless mistakes while publishing their books. In these chapters, we will provide details on different problems that an author might face, and give you innumerable tips on the art of self-publishing and its intricacies. We tell you what to look for when choosing a self-publishing/hybrid publishing company to make sure you don't end up disappointed. We want you to become a #1 bestseller, and we know you can do it.

Writers usually come across two types of terms: "All Rights" and "Work for Hire." When they sign an agreement with a "Work for Hire" clause, they lose not only their rights to a book but the copyright as a whole. The publisher, in this case, will become both the owner and "author."

2. LOST PUBLISHING RIGHTS

– LOSING MIND AND SOUL!

Retaining publishing rights is as important and critical as publishing the book itself. Publishing right is a lifeline for an aspiring author. The right to publish your work is your solitary right to retain the brand identity.

Usually, an author negotiates publishing rights when he or she signs the contract with the publisher. In the past, publishers wanted authors to sign away their contracts before publication and this negative practice hurt authors ability to control or assert their rights. Your rights are invaluable and you must keep the content and distribution of your publication. When you have the rights to your book, you can control the publication pricing! Additionally, you can even control the contents of the book and its distribution to a large group of people around the world. You should negotiate and bargain your way well in advance, and make sure that you discuss this issue with the publisher so that you retain the entire set of copyrights forever.

One of the important questions that every other budding writer wants to ask is "Is it right to sell my rights to the book I am going to publish?" A rather tricky question is difficult to answer at times! When you write a book, you would become the sole copyright holder for your work. You need not register copyright to announce to the world that you own it. However, you should hold the copyright just in case you want to prove a case of copyright infringement by someone at sometime in the future. With the copyright, you will also own a series of other rights that you could sell to others in the future. For example, it is possible to sell or license "First European Serial Rights" to one applicant or allow first online, electronic rights to another. In fact, you can announce a series of different licenses of rights to retain control over the work. To boost sales, you might even give away all reprint rights, republication licenses or translation rights for a specific period! This is another avenue for an additional revenue stream. For instance, the book Rich Dad Poor Dad licensed their book to China and have been getting royalty checks every month. To get a copyright go to copyright.gov and register your book.

By chance, if you sell your rights to the publisher, you will lose your ability to resell or license the material to any other usage forms and with this loss, you are as good as a reader who reads your book! Your publishers will become the default owner of all rights to your own work, and they will grant rights to others at will and with their own discretion. When you demand to hold all rights, you will not lose your copyright. You are still the original author and the publisher will never claim authorship or full rights to the book. But you are now in a partnership with the traditional publishing house and they will also have a say in what goes and what does not go in your book. It's important to know that you may not agree with the editor but they will have final say as to what is best in the book.

Giving away all rights

Many authors take a cautious stand by giving away all rights to their book work. Some compelling reasons may force them to do so and they may not understand the risks and trade-offs involved. The reasons most commonly attributed for ceding all rights include:

Money: An "All Rights" contract may attract a new writer, especially, when he or she is need of money or when a specific piece of work is very hard to market the second time. A number of publishers may also offer a very decent pay out in exchange for an "All Rights" contract.

Name and Prestige: Who does not need name, fame, and prestige? Some best and top of the markets demand all rights in exchange for a perceived prestige and name. First-time authors often believe that publishing in such markets far outweighs the total loss of rights. They also believe that the payment that they receive for forgoing all rights is a sensible decision.

A burning ambition to enter the writer market: A first-time trade-off in the form of an all-rights agreement seems to attract many writers because they merely want to get a foothold in an industry that is full of immense competition. First-time reputation is perhaps the biggest motivation for many writers to concede all rights to their work.

Does it mean that a writer should readily accept these tips to sign an agreement that demands full rights to a book? Alternatively, is there any option left that allows a writer to keep all rights while getting the best bargain in return? As a writer, you will need to be very cautious and well-informed while negotiating a contract. Just consider these simple solutions:

Ask probing questions: First, ask why your publisher needs to own all rights to your work. In many cases, a writer might just get a standard contract – a so-called "no frill" type of contract. It is also very likely that a publisher may propose the same contract for all writers just to reduce their administrative and functional costs down to the minimum. Asking questions about the contract and probing inquiries may push them to agree to most of your conditions and terms.

Stop pleading and never beg: It is possible that your publisher just wants to run you down. More often, publishers think that it is a win-win situation both for them and for the writers – they get their full rights and writers get their payment. It is almost like a level playing field! However, writers always miss something with such a kind offer. Be professional and courteous while forwarding your demand with the publisher. Be firm and never get emotional while forwarding your case.

Be straightforward and do not try to mislead publishers: Never

ever try to mislead your future publisher and do not lie. Many writers try to project the wrong picture that some other publishers are waiting eagerly waiting to publish their books. Just remember that a publisher is highly professional and misleading him or her is almost impossible. Be honest and convey what you really want from your publisher.

It is not a "you or me" type of situation: Life is never a "take it or leave it" kind of game. Publishing is not a competitive game. Try to play an even game. In other words, be ready to give something in exchange for others that you might find very lucrative in the future. Try to negotiate in small increments and parts. Forego some rights while retaining some. It always pays to negotiate with your publisher. Ask them to give you some rights, like electronic or movie/TV rights. Alternatively, you can even argue for a specific geographical right to extend your success in those areas where you feel you can sell more.

Check, negotiate and sign: When doing any publishing deal it is very important to read your contract. Whether you are choosing a self-publishing company that will help you self-publish your book, or you are short-listing a traditional publishing company that will publish your printed book, you will need to read the contract carefully with a magnifying glass in your hand. Make sure that you have rights to the book. Ensure that there are no extra fees for marketing.

Before signing the agreement, check all documents and forms for any hidden clauses that might cajole you to give your consent. Some publishers may simply refuse if you insist on not signing a "give-it-away" type of contract, while others are more willing to negotiate with you. In other words, some traditional publishers are far more flexible in their business approach; they may even allow you to retain full rights to your book. We believe you should retain full rights to your book.

Insist on retaining specific rights: Some publishers do not need full rights for the book that you want to publish. You can always demand from the publishers to retain some of the specific rights that you might consider important for your future. Such rights may include rights of translation, international and geographical rights or even audio and video rights, including possible conversion into movie and audio scripts. This simple approach will also permit you to enforce certain conditions that will help you immensely in the future.

Demand for a full return of rights at a later stage: When a publication is past its print life, the publisher might not consider it as important to retain all rights. You can try to ask your publishers to return some of the specific rights back to you. Asking will never hurt you and a gentle persuasion will go a long way to help you seize some of the ceded initiatives.

Many writers are known to sell all their rights because they feel that there are no other options left. However, it is wise to remember that in today's world self-publishing and hybrid publishers are there to help you get your book published and YOU keep all your rights and ownership.

If you are thinking of giving away all rights to your work, consider the below-mentioned points and evaluate your options. With a traditional publisher will you be happy with:

- Someone else finalizing the content of your book?

- Not being able to log into your Amazon account adjust categories, keywords or optimize your book to boost it to #1 bestseller status?

- Never collecting all the royalties of your book?

- Not being able to make updates at a moment's notice?

- Not being able to control the price?

- Not being able to control the distribution?

Copyrights and their utility in the publication world.

Copyright is a legalized tool to claim a piece of work (like the contents of a book) as your own so that you can ask for damages, if anyone tries to copy the content without your explicit permission. If you are a copyright holder, it will protect both your published and unpublished works from infringements, provided you publish them in an appropriate medium. It is possible for you to register copyrights in order to file a case against someone who infringed your copyrights. In other words, you will need to publish the work in a proper medium that enables you as the legal owner of the copyright. Copyright laws come into force as soon as you register your copyright. Before signing a book deal, ensure that the publisher incorporates essential issues of copyrights to prevent their infringements.

Copyrights offer a number of advantages some of which are listed below:

You can claim authorship for your work. In other words, you can proudly say that you produced a body of work; it could be anything from music, artwork, photography, book, article, blog, white papers, technical papers, and paintings. No one can steal your work nor can one copy you by using another name or alias.

You are the exclusive owner of your work. No one, apart from you, can sell them without your permission. Nobody can even publish them again without your consent. You are the sole authority, who can determine how someone can use your copyright. If someone is interested in using your work, he or she will need your permission to do so.

You have the sole right to license others to use your work. These rights could be publication rights, performance rights, display rights, reprint rights or even playing rights. In some cases, you can allow someone to use your work on a one-time basis.

You will have the right to create derivatives and byproducts of your previously published work. This is true when the author is a fiction book writer. For example, it is easy to use the original character to create another in a sequel or forthcoming part. Creating music or painting as additional offshoots of original work are some of the other areas.

With the published work, you will have the exclusive rights to generate profits and make money. As an intellectual property holder, you will also hold the rights to sell your work to others. In other words, you will earn royalties that can transfer to anyone in your family. In fact, royalties are a residual form of passive income that keeps on coming to you year after year.

Almost all publishers fail to address the concerns of first time authors who want to establish their presence in the publishing world. This is especially true when they deal with different forms of publishing rights. For example, a series of broad categories of rights exist in the publishing world, and a publisher may deny one or many of these rights that are exclusive to you. Here are some of those common rights that you can demand from your publisher:

Media communication: This relates to the ways and methods in which your publisher publishes and distributes materials. Out of the two important media, "print" and "electronic", a publisher may refuse to give away both of these rights to a writer. However, both of them are inclusive of each other. Print publications demand electronic rights and similarly, electronic rights for a piece of work demand print rights. As an author, you should be careful enough to demand both of these rights.

Distribution and delivery: During the days of "print only" publication, writers used to accept serial rights that meant that the distribution rights were solely restricted to a certain geographical region or location. However, with the advent of an electronic and virtual medium, the definition of geographical rights has lost it meaning and readers from all over the world read anything that is published in an electronic format. It also means that a writer should be able to demand both geographical as well electronic rights for their work.

Important points to remember:

Many publication rights are "use" type of rights. So, when publishers use them, they are automatically transferring them immediately after use. For example, the "first rights" in a specific medium, is used just once and it is lost forever for you if you are not careful while negotiating the rights contract with your publisher. However, if you refuse to sign a rights contract, the publisher will not be able to claim a number of other rights.

Never ever, believe publishers when they say that, "all rights will revert to you after publication." Some rights may revert to you, while a host of others will never come to you. When a publisher publishers something, you can never expect the rights to be fully "exclusive" and "selective."

Remember that when an author does not sign to transfer copyrights, he or she will never lose them even after the formal publication. This question simply does not arise, because the publisher can never claim a host of rights because they do not own them.

To sum this up, copyright laws are still the old tools that work, either way, to protect writers' interests or a publisher's commercial gains. It usually cuts and eats into a writer's fortune. At most, many of the copyright laws treat creative works similarly irrespective how and in what manner something is published and distributed. Copyright laws are created to protect your interests. Unfortunately, many publishers try to use them to their advantage by denying rightful ownership of a creative piece of work by original creators. If you are a writer who is trying to publish your first work, be wary of those publishers, who try to hijack your advantages and benefits by denying your basic copyrights. It is best left to your wisdom to find an appropriate publishing agency that takes care of your interests and commercial outlook.

3. Speed over Quality

There are a number of ways of not doing something! Similarly, you can find a number of ways of doing stupid things too! More often, people tend to ask, "what if I publish a book within a month or so?" Equally, there are writers who are in a real haste to publish something that is beyond their actual capability. Some writers even go the extent of hiring someone to do the spadework, so that they can save precious time. However, things never turn out the way you want them to be! Publishing a book is just like producing something in a production facility. It is just like an expensive car coming out of an assembly plant that uses a highly sophisticated process chain that depends on periodic quality checks and assessment points.

In the publishing world, the most critical issue that writers overlook is the speed at which a book is written, formatted, proofread, printed and published. A publisher is always in a hurry to produce more books in the shortest possible time. In fact, it is crucial for them to print as many books as possible to create a big stream of income. They also compare the speed with which big publishers mass-produce books for the reading public. Almost all well-known publishers have the ability to produce thousands of titles in a year. However, can an individual writer publish his or her book at the same speed? It is almost impossible for an individual writer to publish that many books in the same way.

Speed can kill! This is especially, true in the publishing world. Speed is the number one enemy of quality! Speed and high-quality work can never go together. Both of them are inversely proportional; more speed means inferior quality, while reasonable speed signifies better quality. Both speed and quality can never intersect each other. What you deliver to your reader is as important as any other thing. Speed can ruin your work! Unreasonable speed can force you to commit hundreds of mistakes and big blunders. Speed should overtake professionalism, precision, completeness, finesse, and perfection.

Every work of creative art has its shelf life. Now, writing is a creative art of the highest order. There is an organized process involved in the publishing industry. Each step of publishing is a laborious process and you must complete every one of them in order to reach the top. In other words, every step involved in publishing has a definite purpose. It has its own time frame that you cannot ignore as a writer. A high-quality publication usually takes three to five months to complete.

There are several reasons why you should pick quality over the speed with which you want to publish your work. Some of them are as follows:

Obviously, you wish for a very high-quality product. A high-quality product is only possible when you consider the content, format, type set, photographs, style and presentation of the book. You might need to learn how to draw a fine, thin line between the factors of speed and quality. You may also need to find out how you can produce a top class product in the fastest possible time frame. The most important issue is to publish a book in the quickest possible time without losing overall quality.

As mentioned before, speed can kill your hard-earned effort. Surely, it can spoil everything that eventually leads to failure of the product. A simple mistake can cost you many things; a badly produced book can reduce the overall marketability of the book. Here is a simple example of how you can destroy your effort within a day or two. Let us assume that you have a great plot and storyline for your book. Now, you begin creating a broad layout for your book, its covers, and title. The extreme hurry with which you are trying to publish your book may spoil your party! Once, you are ready with your content and book format, your next step is to proofread and edit the content, so that all formatting and language errors are eliminated. However, the extreme haste may drive you to commit the first mistake. The first casualty that every writer faces in a lifetime is a badly proofread and edited manuscript!

Nearly all commonly occurring mistakes and blunders that you might commit during your journey as an established author are as follows (most of them occur when you are in a hurry to publish your book):

- Low quality cover art and graphics
- Poor proofreading and editing
- Incorrect formatting
- Wrong chapter layout
- Bad content
- Poor use of type-setting and fonts
- Very poor preparation before launching
- No social media promotion
- No pre-publication marketing campaign
- Relying excessively on the speed of publication which leads to failure

A road map to better publication – Speed and quality in perfect harmony

It is possible to publish a great piece of work in the quickest possible time all the while maintaining a high quality of production. Book publication is a series of different steps that eventually lead to the final publication stage when you are ready to taste success. What are the major publication steps that you should do in order to create a successful book? Here are some critical steps that you should take when publishing books. Make sure that you give due attention to each step based on your needs, requirements, and priorities. The following schematic diagram gives you a flowchart and a clear bird's eye view of different publishing steps:

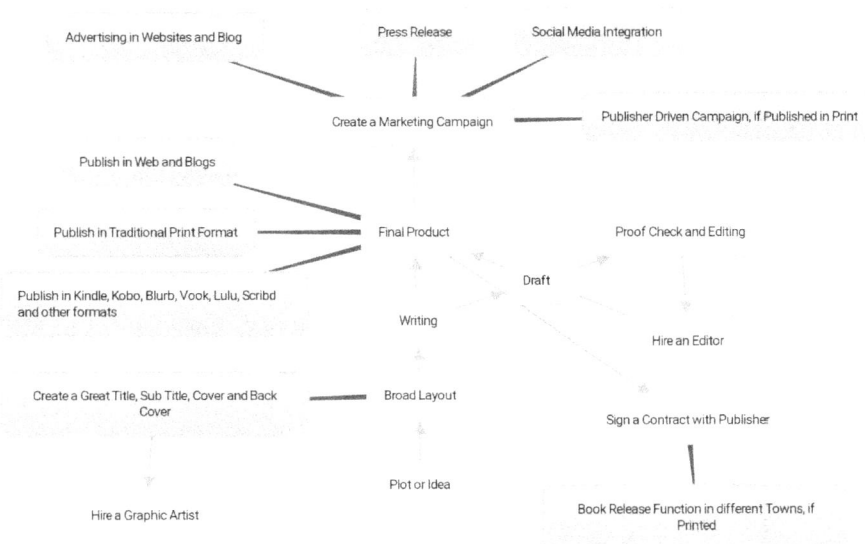

Writing the parts of a book are very simple if you have a solid storyline or theme in your mind. In the absence of it, a writer would waste more time, effort and energy; an incomplete plot might drag your writing plan by weeks, if not months. Many authors' common complaint is "I could have finished my book, only if I had more time!" In effect, they usually complain that they do not have enough time to finish their book and publish. The relationship between time and the completion of a book always feels tricky and challenging. It can either hold you back in your work or propel you forward towards quicker completion and eventual publication. Time is relative and it provides you a level playing field; it is up to your wisdom to finish your work quickly or just wait patiently enough to create a faultless work.

Time management is key to everything. It is just like driving a car and reaching a destination; the driver applies his or her wisdom and sense of timing to either go fast or slow to reach the destination. Excessive speed can kill a driver. Similarly, snail-like speed can lead to other complications that are as important as well. In the world of publication, you may have to draw a fine line of balance to distinguish between speed and quality. Both of them are important and critical to your success.

"The first draft of everything is shit."
-Ernest Hemingway

Once you finish writing, the next very important step is to create a manuscript or draft. An important part of the publishing process, this is the step where a majority of writers fail in their attempt to deliver a high-quality product. The manuscript or draft stage also consumes a lot of time, due to proofreading and editing; in fact, the back and forth time taken by the draft depends on the speed with which your editor/ proof checker works and delivers progress reports. Similarly, the time taken by you to send your comments on the proofreading checks is also vital. While finalizing a draft, it is possible to reduce the overall amount of time taken from the first stage to the last.

For example, a tried and trusted formula articulates that a second draft must be about 10% shorter and leaner than the first. The third one should be 10% shorter than the second version and this workflow should be maintained until you feel that you have a workable draft in hand. This approach not only saves precious time but also provides a high-quality product; this method also helps you bring a great deal of clarity to the storyline, as well as improve the overall pacing of the draft proofreading and editing. Self-publishing is usually faster than the traditional publishing, because you are the sole decision-making entity, while a team always looks after your project in the case of traditional publishing.

The time taken to repair, edit and proofread the first draft is much more than the time duration that you invest on subsequent versions of improvised drafts. To save time, speed up things and to enhance quality, weed out unnecessary jargon, complicated words, and sentences, simplify and reduce the length of the sentences, and edit the entire manuscript for a clean flow. This approach will help you in spending much lesser time on subsequent drafts that are leaner, meaner and more meaningful. As much as possible, insist on your proofreading expert to adhere to a tougher delivery schedule; however, never push him or her too hard, so that the quality of work dips to a low standard.

With the third improvised draft, you should have a highly polished manuscript that you can dispatch to your editor. Creating a catchy title and colorful back and front cover are mandatory too for a bestselling book. You will have to align and complete this work with the proofreading project, and both of them should run concurrently to save time, energy and speed up the overall schedule. Again, outsource the work to a professional graphic artist who can finish the work within a tight time frame. Creating a title, back page synopsis, prologue and epilogue should not take much time because of your close acquaintance with the storyline and subject matter.

Probably, the biggest hurdles to the publication of a book are learning how to self-publish or finding someone to help you self-publish, someone who is ready to publish your book, execute marketing campaigns, help you promote and eventually boost you up to bestseller. There are many hybrid publishers in the world today. Companies or individuals that can self-publish your book for you while you keep all the rights and royalties. In the meanwhile, you may want to monitor the progress of proofreading of the draft by including editing and grammar checks. If you are outsourcing the work to a freelancer or a professional proofreader, you should insist on a rigid period for timely delivery and satisfactory result. Ensure that the manuscript undergoes at least three rounds of proofreading checks. Assign time for each round of checks and give a day's rest to your proof checker; this allows him or her to start fresh and with a pair of new eyes. Calculate the total time needed to complete at least three rounds of checks and create a timeline. The first draft need not be the perfect draft; invariably, it will have plenty of mistakes and grammatical errors. Authors who choose a self-publishing company should have the luxury of speed to the market place. Which is a huge advantage over choosing the traditional publishing route.

All books can be published in two different ways: traditional printing and self-publication (also called Indie and POD publishing). A book could be self-published under many platforms and different companies. Some of the most popular platforms are Kindle Direct Publishing, Blurb publishing, Elite Online Publishing, CreateSpace, IngramSpark, Nook Press, Kobo Writing Life, Smashwords, BookBaby, Author House, Nu Book and Fast Pencil. These options are excellent and results-oriented, because the book publication is quite a bit cheaper and ultra quick, while the publishers themselves offer book promotion and marketing. This will help save invaluable time and you can easily divert the time saved to enhance the quality of your final product.

A successful book launch is not possible without launching a faultless and efficient marketing campaign. In fact, this very delicate and sensible operation requires the investment of a fair amount of time, energy, money and effort. You can effortlessly launch a sustained marketing promotion and campaign in two different ways: by using a print medium or by hosting it on social media. A publisher seldom uses a marketing campaign by print medium these days, because it is expensive in the first place and it may not reach a large group or targeted audience. However, publishers and authors can still advertise in special supplements of newspapers and magazines in the form of book launch announcements, reviews, and critiques.

Social media campaigning is the quickest possible tool available to publishing houses and authors. A solid level playing field, social media can help them in many ways like:

Reaching thousands of social media influencers that are active in online forums, chats and message threads.

To save time, effort and energy, decide on your target market depending on demography, readership, cost, and budget. These approaches will help you immensely if you are a self-publisher. The main objective is to reach numerous readers in the shortest possible time.

To gather momentum in terms of time and money, you should plan well ahead of the launch schedule. Establish your presence on all major social media websites and book promotion portals. There are many of them and you can use these forums to spread the news about the product launch.

Offline networks are the most underestimated media channels! Make sure that you use them for maximum effect. For example, traditional publishers ask all authors to answer an Author Questionnaire that gives valuable tips and resources to tap the local and global marketing opportunities. Offline media tools may also include tv spots, podcasts, radio shows, chat strings, college and community magazines or local press releases.

Book trailers, chapter snippets, previews are some interesting tools that you can use as promotional tools.

Targeted emails can reach thousands of readers at a time and you may need to contact a professional agency to send out emails to your list.

Publish articles about your book by contacting professional bloggers, who permit writers to post them as guest writers. In other words, become a guest author to write on something whose topic is closest to your book.

Book festivals (online and offline) are excellent forums, where you can distribute fliers that highlight the summary of your book.

Develop an inspiration for generating new ideas. As Jack London told us, *"You can't wait for inspiration. You have to go after it with a club."* After all, it is your project and the book is your baby. Go ahead, nurture it and let it grow in an international market!

You have to read every sentence of your book. You are supposed to know exactly what is in your book. It is very simple

> — *If you do not have time to read, you do not have the time or the tools to write (Stephen King).*

In other words, you should know every scene and plot of the book. It is likely that you will speak more about your book during your book launch party.

The above-mentioned tips and suggestions are likely to help you in ensuring high quality of the book and they could assist you in your struggle towards publishing a book too. If you are using these tips, you can effortlessly integrate impeccable quality into the final product all the while saving precious time, energy and effort. Also, keep in mind that you are writing on your own and if you are a self-publisher, you will be writing on your own dime too! Saving time and holding on to the quality are two separate things and you should consider different factors to retain them both.

4. NO MARKETING SUPPORT

– MISSING THE PATH TO FORTUNE!

Almost all new authors believe that their newfound traditional publishers simply go out of their way to promote books. However, this belief seems to be far-fetched from actual truth and it is rarely the case too. You may not know that most of them have very tight marketing budgets and whatever they have at their disposal, they will reserve it for a few of their celebrity authors. New authors also find themselves at their loose ends to find a way to promote their books apart from minuscule marketing effort offered by publishers. The minimum most marketing campaigns that a publisher will perform is listing books in the book catalog and sending promotional mail fliers to libraries and book buying resources; as an author, you can expect this basic paraphernalia and this is where the adventure ends. Yes, a publisher might help you find your book in a local library! Do not forget that it is not just enough to sell your book! Book sales in today's digitized world take place through online buying and here your publisher will not try hard enough to promote your books.

To remind you, bookstores are never the selling points that guarantee you a major portion of sales. The shelf life of your book on a bookshelf of a bookstore is just a few months and bookstore owners stock a few copies of your book. If your book does not do well, they are more likely to return your title to your publishers and seek refunds from them. If this is the case, your book is as good as dead even before its arrival in the market. There are two reasons why traditional sellers often fail to sell books in a bookstore: bookstores use two selling models called "pay-to-play" and "play-to-galleries." In the former case, bookstores tend to pay their publishers for only those books that sell in large numbers; otherwise, they will return those books that do not sell at all. In the latter case, bookstores accommodate those authors who are already well known, recognized and identified in the publication world. In other words, bookstores are likely to sell books of such authors who have a proven sales history and good selling record. Traditional publishers usually assign a media consultant or a "publicist", who can try to get a foothold in the book market. However, this service is very disappointing, as you may just get a few numbers of blog submissions or a single radio or community interview that usually ends up in a big failure.

In the end, publishers want authors who can negotiate with a solid and pre-planned 'promotional platform"; this means that your publishers will expect you to come to them with a "predefined" and "already existing" market base that can buy your book! Certainly, publishers want to mitigate their risk levels and they want a "ready-to-read" market that can buy books as soon as a title is released. During the signing process, your publisher would like to know the kind of marketing support that you assign to your book. Some publishers may even suggest you invest some money in marketing aspects of publishing. Even if you ask them to match your amount with theirs, they may not budge and simply refuse to consider your request for a matching amount. This "take-it-or-leave-it" attitude on the part of the publisher may leave you in the lurch. Therefore, you might need to assess and evaluate whether to find a traditional publisher or go for self-publishing.

All publishers basically love to think that marketing is the brain that propels their publishing business. They also feel that marketing support and campaign are the two important parts of the brain that move their idea of marketing. Marketing and sales departments of any publishing house will have two areas of duties – promotion and sales. In the meanwhile, sales are further divided into different departments, where marketing department will include other sub-houses like promotion, publicity, advertising, sales to selling chains, sales to institutions, libraries and individuals, bookstores, translations and subsidiary/copyright departments.

Normally, publishing houses usually depend on two modes of marketing tools to promote a book: advertising and publicity. In the normal course, advertising is a mode of placement of expensive print and virtual ads in online or offline resources like newspapers, magazine, journals, websites, blog and online advertising streams. This approach solely focuses on promoting the author as well as the publishers at the same time; publishers believe that this will assist them to gain additional focus and attention, than the one that is secured by the author. In reality, advertising is very expensive and publishers may never cede this unique space to new authors or to those whose earlier publications have failed to reach their expectations. On the contrary, people naturally confuse the term publicity with that of advertising! In fact, both of them are quite different. Here, publicity is *"hear us"* or *"look at us"* kind of a publishing campaign. In reality, this mode of marketing is much more powerful than any other kind, because publishers always work with TV, newspapers and internet media to send messages across about a specific publication. In the normal course, publicity departments also deal with book launch functions, tours, events, parties, interviews, TV book talks and author autograph events.

Again, this privilege is reserved only for established authors and new ones may not get such a royal treatment. If the publisher feels that your book is marketable, then you may get some portions of their budget towards dedicated publicity. However, the chances are quite remote because the publisher will still have to spend money on this exercise. There are reasons why a publisher hesitates to publicize your book: the need to spend even before your book is released, and the lingering fear that your book may not do well in the market. Here is an example of how publicity budget is fixed for your book.

Let us assume that your book does well and sell enough copies to bring sales of about $100,000. Based on this assumption, the publisher will fix an investment of 15% of $100,000 towards marketing and publicity; this comes to about $15,000. The publisher has a unique problem in hand because spend it in a whole chunk even before your book is released and marketed. If your book sells well in the market, you can expect sales of $100,000 and this will justify the public investment of $15,000. Otherwise, this will be a dead investment, the publisher will simply stop paying attention to your book, and the book will join the queue of failed projects. This is why you cannot expect a traditional publisher to help you market your book!

Here are some harsh truths about traditional publishers and the process with a new author:

Publicity budget is just a small part of the amount that the publisher spends towards publicity.

It is you, who count for them. If you are a new author, you can expect little cooperation from your publisher. Conversely, chances of getting your share of publicity budget are very remote!

If you are a first-time author, your book may not bring name and fame to you and your publisher! It might be just your enthusiasm driving you forward and not the publisher! Your publisher may never have the same kind of enthusiasm for your book!

Almost all publishers want you to take care of your book promotion, marketing, and publicity. If you are ready to spend a huge amount of money, then they may partner with you to publicize and promote your book. In other words, it is just "other people's money" for your publisher!

Time is of the essence here! If you want to publish a book, you may have to complete your book at least 6 months before the publication date. All publishers officially publish two catalogs of their books, one during the fall and the other during spring. Just make sure that you fit into this calendar without fail. Still, famous publishers may try to postpone or give you a very long publication schedule for the forthcoming book just because you are new and unknown to them.

Is your book presentable to readers? One of the significant mistakes committed by publishers is the pre-conceived idea that your book is not good or sometimes unfit for the market. It is often a stereotypical belief on the part of many publishers to form an opinion about the book even before it is printed and released. This is more damaging to authors than any other issues.

Simply speaking, traditional publishing is hard. If you are lucky, you may get a decent and reasonable publisher, who is ready to spend some money to promote and publicize your book. Alternatively, you may never get a good one, who can treat you on the same level playing field as other successful writers. Most probably, you will hardly find a good publisher who can satisfy your needs and requirements. In other words, you may need to find a way of finding your own well-crafted book-marketing plan that will help sell a decent number of copies.

If you are choosing a traditional publisher, you might choose the one who provides you a clear-cut marketing blueprint. Without a solid blueprint, do not sign the contract straight away. Rather, you should argue your way to find a good and workable blueprint. Here are some of the points that you should consider while choosing a publisher:

Industry standard, marketing blueprints offer a six to twelve-month online marketing campaign, plus publicity and promotional strategies for the lifetime of the book. Insist on a marketing plan for your book.

Invariably, any book would need three types of support – pre-launch, launch and post-launch support to ensure complete visibility for the book. Most publishers ignore the first part because it involves spending a large amount of money. You should argue with the publisher to secure all three of these activities so that you will stand on a profitable playing field.

Ask the publisher to claim and optimize your Amazon author page, that allows readers to notice your presence online and know more about you.

If you fail to get a fair deal from the traditional publisher, you may try out self-publishing as a tool to publish the book. However, you still have to market it, even if you are planning to launch the book through a self-publishing portal. Some of the most critical works you create start much before you finish writing. You should consider the following two important issues before marketing book through self-publishing:

The reasons and needs for which you are writing.

What benefits will you offer your readers or what are the positive things that your audience is going to get after reading the book?

Note: These two issues will drive your book marketing strategies for the future. Also, note that the extent or degree of marketing effort that you put also depend on these factors.

Further, if you are an author and if you want to market your book through self-publishing and find that….

- You do not have a stable marketing plan to launch the book…
- You have been receiving a wrong hearing by your traditional publisher or…
- You are planning to write a book, but do not know how to publish and market it through the self-publishing route…

Here is information that will help you achieve your marketing goals and objectives. Don't forget there are book marketing companies ready to help you launch your book to bestseller status. With the right team, your book can become a bestseller.

You may hesitate to launch your self-published book without a proper and comprehensive marketing plan! Use a detailed marketing checklist, before you release your book to the big world of publishing. You should stick to your marketing plan even against all odds and without fail.

If you don't launch a book with a proper marketing plan the following could happen:

- You might lose your money or you may not show an ROI on your book.
- You could miss the first-week promotion that boosts your sales.
- You may also fail to gather the names and emails of your readers.
- You might overlook setting up JV partners who could help you promote the book.

What exactly is a marketing plan?

A marketing plan is a clearly defined blueprint, a guide, or a checklist to meander through each, individual stage of the book launch. The eventual goal of a marketing plan is to pass and sell the book to as many readers as possible and in the process make enough money, name, and fame. The book also represents your marketing plan which would characterize the level of success that it will achieve post-launch.

There are two ways of marketing your book – online marketing and offline marketing. Nothing beats the magic of creating a blog/website to market and publicize your book. It is the right time to create your own website or blog to advertise your book. If you do not have one, go ahead and create it. To use blog and websites, you should also learn how internet technology works and in what manner you can use social media platforms in conjunction with your main website. If you are not a technical person, great news, you can hire a web designer for a minimal cost. However, it is imperative that you would use the magic of digital technology to advertise the book on the World Wide Web.

On the other hand, off-site marketing deals with all techniques and strategies other than the ones that you deploy on a virtual medium. It may include TV/Radio interview and advertisements, podcast interviews, chat shows, book launch events, book signing events, lecture circuits, speaking to readers, newspaper interviews, sending out postal fliers, booklets and brochures, library meetings and many other such events. Nevertheless, these are more expensive options than online advertising, and they take a longer duration to reach intended readers. In addition, you will be forced to spend a lot of time, effort and energy.

A Simple Book Marketing Plan

The following steps will help you streamline your marketing plan and get your book ready to market.

Main Purpose

The purpose for which you wrote your book is perhaps the foundation stone for the entire exercise. You may need to ask yourself some questions like "what am I promoting?" and "where does my book fit into and what would be the most appropriate genre?" When you write the main purpose, you can make things easier and simpler. The next question is to ask how an actionable plan could be set in place to generate more leads and grow your list of potential readers who can not only read your book but also promote it to others. This will naturally lead to another important question, "what is the next step when I launch my book?" You will want to sell more books by creating a buzz, and you can raise the book sales by using various marketing techniques by deploying both online, and offline plans. Another question to ask is "what is the call to action in the book?" What do you want the reader to do after they are done reading your book? Do you have a product or service you can sell to them? Can you create one?

Target Market

Once you have the book ready, you may want to define the target market where you wish to sell the book. In fact, your target market is identifying the idea of a model reader who is more likely to read the book. This is perhaps the most important step in the marketing process because once you identify who reads your book, you will be able to fine-tune the entire process. Reaching target market is an exhaustive process because you will contact hundreds of people in person or on the internet. You may also contact people through your mailing list. To create a buzz around the book, you will have to raise use numerous publishing platforms like Amazon Kindle, Nook, or CreateSpace. The most significant advantages of publishing on these no-frill and easy-to-do-yourself platforms are instant visibility and identification. In addition, you may also advertise your book to attract a large market of readers who are located online in thousands of websites and blogs.

Here are some important additional tips that you can use to reach your target market:

Offering Kindle or other ebooks formats for some of the readers free of cost will help you get honest online feedback.

You could purchase cheaper advertisement credits from sites like BookBub.com and BookGorilla.com to drive online traffic to your ebook selling page. Review websites and book websites along with a quick blog tour (where you can post guest blogs highlighting the main features of your book) will also help you gather additional traffic.

The promotion week will begin within the first week after you release your book. Use ebook publication platforms that are listed above.

Social media is a very powerful tool that can assist reach thousands of people with book promotion messages. Social media posts to friends and acquaintances on Twitter, Facebook, Instagram, Pinterest, Google+, LinkedIn, WhatsApp, GoodReads, StumbleUpon and other social media platforms will strengthen your overall marketing strategy.

If you have a video blog, it is possible to broadcast video messages to your readers. Otherwise, you may also write a written blog to put views simultaneously across to a large number of readers. If you have influential contacts within your reach, make sure to ask them to help you give an interview to radios, TV, and podcasts. Write down the most important questions about the book and ask the interviewer to pose these questions to you.

In many cases, writers will host a blog on the upcoming book, highlight some important points, distribute preview e-copies of books to select readers and send flyers to people on the mailing lists. You may also require to host this blog three months before the launch and continue it for at least 3 months after the launch. Promote the blog to create a big mailing list. Publish a chapter preview of the book on your blog. Ask people to comment on it; make sure that people who comment are signing into your opt-in mailing list.

Facebook promotion: Announce the arrival of the book on your personal fan page at least three months before the launch of the book. Publish periodic updates about the launch and promote the book by sending e-version of the first chapter to all readers. Use your wall effectively to reach interested groups and forums that exist on Facebook. If you have enough financial resources, you could even spend some money on Facebook advertisements by creating a page for the book. Publish a landing page link to go directly to your blog where readers can order copies of the book.

Twitter conversations: Twitter, a microblogging site, is an excellent tool to spread messages across to many people, who are more likely to re-tweet the same message to their friends and acquaintances. Send a series of tweets to advertise the book. Publish a real-time Twitter text widget on your blog to let people see what is happening on Twitter. Post about the book for at least one to three months before the launch.

Ask your followers to re-tweet messages to reach their contacts. Publish links to landing pages and book buy page of the blog.

Word of mouth is the best tool: Request your friends, acquaintances, and relatives to post links about the book on their social media pages. Words of mouth are possibly the best words that humans can speak! They can raise the sales of the book and help establish a brand for your book. Word of mouth has a cascading effect that is deep and wide. In fact, it is geometrically progressive in its nature and it can reach hundreds of people within a few numbers of days.

Apart from the above-mentioned action plan tips, you may also create a "to-do" schedule to track events just before and after the launch of the book. Here are some more tips that will help you create a solid marketing plan:

- Finalize both versions of the book – print and ebook .
- Send advance and sample digital copies to select readers.
- Keep in contact with them throughout the pre-launch and post-launch of the book.
- Just before the actual launch, try to give at least 10 interviews in a week to different sources as mentioned above.
- Purchase and print and virtual ad spaces to post messages about the book. Use most popular tools like a blog and social media platforms.
- Submit 10 or more blog posts and announce the actual launch date for the book.
- Seek interview opportunities (at least 10) by contacting different media channels.

- Publish daily tweets and postings on Twitter, Facebook, StumbleUpon and other popular platforms.
- Start sending emails to your list before and after the book launch. They should be qualified and interested in reading your book.
- Write guest posts on popular sites and ask readers to write reviews. Ensure that you send links to them to download a chapter preview copy.
- Just before (at least 30 days) the book launch, publish your final version of the Kindle ebook on Amazon. Let people buy e-versions of the book and spread the word around. Many authors usually publish their first Kindle copies just a day prior to the actual launch of the print version. However, many others just publish their Kindle and other self-published copies and forget about releasing hardback or paperback copies. This might be a wise decision because many recognized publishers usually develop an interest in buying the full rights for the printed version. For example, Crown Publishing decided to buy Andy Weir's self-published book titled, The Martian for $100,000. Another memorable example is James Redfield's bestseller book titled, The Celestine Prophecy.
- If you are self-publishing your book, you can head straight to any of the smaller bookstores and become acquainted with the owners. This way, you can meet many readers in the bookstore who may buy your book in the bookstore itself.

First-time authors usually find publishing their book a horrendous experience! Most of them are in a dilemma whether to look for a traditional publisher or find a self-publishing platform. If you get great marketing support from a traditional publisher, just go ahead and grab it. Otherwise, you can always self-publish your book and get help from a hybrid publisher or book marketing expert. Good marketing effort is necessary for successful selling of your book and you may create one, even if you are selling on a traditional platform or a self-publishing one. It is worth it!

5. Focusing Only On Print

– Misplaced Priorities can Hurt!

One of the fatal mistakes that many first time authors commit is focussing only on the print editions of their book. Print editions are great! They look and feel very good with their colorful front and back covers. When your first print copy arrives in the mail, you will definitely dance with sheer joy and excitement. You might even feel the pain and frustration that you experienced all through the days when you were waiting for the print edition to appear. As an author, you have an unlimited number of options to publish your book. The most obvious choice that one usually considers is the traditional printing route. However, it is not easy to get your book a publication date with a traditional publisher. Even when you get one, an inordinate wait might test the level of your patience and endurance.

Although traditional publishing is very good, it comes with its own set of rules, regulations, and disadvantages. With traditional publishing, the manuscript might take months and years to become a bound book. You would also need to send the manuscript to several publishing houses and each one of them may take up to eight months to check the contents; this exercise would alone force you to wait in the queue before a getting a positive answer. Even when a publishing house decides to pick your manuscript, it may take another year to publish the book (consider the entire process of checking the draft multiple times plus the actual printing time).

In other words, publishing a book is out of your control when you submit it to one of the traditional publishing houses. Although the content of the book is yours and it is under your control, the editor may suggest hundreds of edits, corrections, and rectifications to your manuscript even when the book does not require them. Unless your work is faultless and even if it meets publishers' in-house guidelines, you may be forced to endure months of rejection and dejection. Now a day, publishers never accept manuscripts directly from the authors and you will need an agent to pass your manuscript to the publishing house. Literary agents usually demand up to 20% cut from author's earning.

On the other hand, self-published books are the fastest way to show and demonstrate your creative potential. Furthermore, authors could easily manage publishing related issues like planning, editing, and marketing. As described before in the previous chapter, retention of full rights becomes very difficult when you negotiate a book deal with your publisher. On the contrary, all rights to self-published books belong to you, you can do whatever you want with your book at any time, and you will escape the constraints placed by the publishers very easily.

Book marketing is the heart and soul of publishing. Without proper marketing support, your book may never sell the way you wanted it to be. Publishers may not be able to devote much time or sufficient money to promote a new author and in the process, the entire book marketing process suffers the most, eventually resulting in very poor sales. In the case of self-publishing, the whole book marketing operation is designed and executed by you. There are plenty of opportunities to sell your books online. The numbers of books that you sell depend on the extent of marketing support you lend to your book. In a previous survey conducted by the Cisco Systems, the overall numbers of web surfers will rise to 25 billion by 2025 and this would result in online revenue of more than $3 trillion. Just imagine the potential of the future market! In effect, book marketing could be an exciting adventure in the future.

If you publish the book only in the print form, you will suffer financially if it fails to sell. Publishers never like a book that fails to sell. In fact, they may simply take the books off the shelves and replace them with other authors who sell well. Publishers also hate excess inventories and they may offer the book for sale at deeply discounted prices that usually results in the loss of royalty income to the author.

This also means that a failed book will report plenty of returns in the form of unsold inventories. This may result in a big failure and utter disappointment! Therefore, you should never rely only on the print versions of the book.

Traditional publishing, in the form of printed versions, offers fewer royalties to authors who usually look for a bigger share of income. The royalty payment is the money given to the author based on a certain percentage of the cover price. For every sale of one copy of the book, the publisher will agree to pay a certain percentage of money to the author. Most generous royalty rate offered to top end authors are about 25%, while fresh and first-time authors may just get a 7-10% royalty rate. This is actually far lesser considering the extent of the effort, energy and monetary resources that you invest in your book. The print-only platform and its royalty calculations are very hard to understand and forecasting an assured cash flow are very difficult too.

Alternatively, book publishing in diverse formats like Kindle and others (usually e-format) offer a steady, definite and assured royalty income. This income is usually on the higher side, because of the lower costs involved in the publication process. As an author, you should never agree to print-only versions of your book. Rather, you might ask the traditional publisher to sell the book on diverse platforms and in different versions so that you can have a bigger share of the income. If the publisher does not agree with this suggestion, you may want to explore the possibility of self-publishing the book.

Why do traditional publishers insist only on printed books

Not all traditional publishers publish books on diverse platforms and in different formats. Most of them publish books in e-format only through their website and buyers will have to pay and download the book from their purchase page. Though, some well-known publishers like Hachette Group allow readers to buy e-formatted books from other web portals like Amazon. Most publishers have their ebook selling web pages that permit readers to pay, download and read. Some examples are Hachette Group, HarperCollins and Penguin Random House. Many publishing houses still love to publish print editions of the book because of the following reasons:

They force authors to cede full book rights to their full advantage. First-time authors are always edgy and apprehensive of possible failures and they are in a hurry to publish their books even when publishers demand full rights. Small upfront payments as advances, also lure first-time authors to concede full rights to their books.

Traditional publishing is after all a big corporate business. Publishers always expect to make money from selling books, even if they have to squeeze authors for their book rights and royalties. If an author fails to understand this logic, he or she may be in a big trouble.

Out of 100 books printed and published, big publishing houses usually incur financial losses in at least 80% of the books. This forces them to be extremely cautious while negotiating contracts with authors.

Print only books in any format are always expensive and the sale volumes of these books are witnessing a steep decline in recent years.

Book debuts usually fail, when they try to sell printed versions of their books online unless the quality and content of the book are of very superior standard. When a printed book fails to go off the shelves through assured sales, book retailers may decide to order only cheaper versions of the book and in very limited numbers.

There is a visible paradox in today's traditional publishing world. A printed book could have a great review, standard marketing campaign, very high quality, an excellent ebook sales figure, yet it may report very low sales volume because of some unknown reasons. This contradiction may force first-time authors and their publishers to look out for logical and specific answers that are difficult to evaluate and analyze.

It is obvious that you will need to establish your author presence in smaller stages and well-calibrated steps. Definitely, starting with cheaper versions of ebooks is a very simple and practical solution. With this innovative approach, you can draw an anxious book buyer to buy from you. In the meanwhile, sufficient sales of the ebook may result in the printing of low priced trade paperbacks; at times, a publisher may express a desire to print, publish and market the ebook in printed format. Eventually, this book conversion may prove very successful, commercial venture for both you and the publisher.

If possible, ensure that you retain ebook rights, while signing a print book contract with a traditional publisher.

In other words, you should be able to find a traditional publisher, who is ready to publish your book in ebook and print formats in different selling platforms like Amazon, Alibris, Barnes, and Noble. If this option is not available to you, you can go ahead and self-publish the book.

In the digital era of self-publication, selling print-only books appears to be a lesser profitable idea. When you sign the book contract with traditional publishers, you can just hope for a 10% royalty income for printed books. If at all they agree to publish and market your book in an ebook format, you may get a maximum royalty rate of 25%. Over time, traditional publishers have learned the art of surviving in a cutthroat industry by maneuvering authors' bargaining power for rights and royalties. To become a successful author, a need arises to market and sell more books. Usually, traditional book publishers consider a sales figure of 5000 and above for printed copies a commercial success. Strangely, not many authors sell more than 500 printed books unless they are well known and bestselling authors. Even if you sell 500 copies of printed books in a year, you can expect an income of around $7000 per year that is very poor by any standard! If you are planning to make a lot of money from a printed book, be ready to sell up to as many as 10,000 copies.

Maybe, it is possible that the era of traditional printing of books is near ending. For this reason, most of them are converting themselves into a hybrid business model, where they publish and sell books in all formats and platforms. In fact, they are offering a six-figure book deal to some proven self-published authors. If you are an independent, self-published author, this could be the golden moment to publish a book that could become a bestseller. Most of the traditional publishers would not want to lose their established business which explains the reasons why they are opening up their business for self-published and Indie authors.

A self-publication firm may offer a hybrid royalty of 20% for printed books and 50% of ebooks and audiobooks. Let us presume that you sell almost 5,000-6,000 copies of both (a split of 50% - 50%). Now, you would earn about $13,000 in royalties that are almost two times more than the ones that you make from a traditional print publisher. These scenarios change remarkably when you decide to self-publish the book. A comparative analysis would reveal that you will earn the best ever royalty rates when you self-publish. Under normal circumstances, you may earn up to 50% on print books and 70% royalty on ebooks. For example, if you manage to sell 5,000 copies (a split of 50% and 50%), the royalty earning could reach $35,000 to $36,000 that is comparable to the best royalty rate paid to celebrity authors. This is a huge upcoming market too. Traditional publishers realize this aspect and they have started offering a hybrid and an imprint selection, where authors could enjoy both printed and virtual editions of books.

Authors, who chose a traditional platform to publish books, may not emerge commercially successful in making money through printed books. Surprisingly, they fail to earn any money because a majority of books never really earns the actual advance amount paid to the author. Countless traditional authors receive an advance payment up-front even before the book is released. This advance payment is misleading at the most, as it is the money given in advance out of the future royalties that are payable to the author. In fact, any upfront advance given to authors must sell enough copies to match it. Otherwise, authors may see a trickle of royalty income for all future sales after the up-front payment. Here is an example to illustrate this scenario:

Let us assume that a celebrity author publishes a novel and the publishing house pays the author $100,000 as an advance. Let us also imagine that the cover price of the book is $20, while the royalty rate is 10%. If the publisher sells 20,000 copies of the book, the total sales volume will be $400,000. Therefore, the author will earn a royalty amount of $40,000. However, the author is already paid an advance amount of $100,000 and this will result in a negative balance of $60,000. The publisher will bear the loss of $60,000, as the author need not pay back the negative balance. Suppose, the book sells 50,000 copies, then the author would earn back the total royalty paid (10% of 50,000 x $20). Any sales above 50,000 copies will earn the author a royalty amount of $2 per book while considering the royalty rate of 10%. However, chances of an author making a huge amount of money from print publications are very bleak. Hence, a prospective author should not focus only print publication; rather, the objective should be selling both ebooks and printed books.

Traditional publishers are very smart! They usually operate on the razor's edge and survive only by selling a few numbers of bestsellers. An occasional "50 Shades of Grey" will always make up for losses incurred on a number of low-advance handouts to lesser-known authors. Another fact to note is that they make money even before you do! Even if a distributor demands 60% of the sale price, the publisher still makes a decent profit at around 25% to 30% (here, the author will get just 10%). Do printed books sell? It is a very difficult question to answer, as the sale volume depends entirely on a number of factors like author's reputation, marketability, and content of the book. However, proper sales support and market effort may yield in a sales volume of 500 copies to 100,000 copies. A rookie author may never sell so much because a traditional publisher usually caters to those authors, who have a considerable social media presence, as well as a solid marketing plan that works to publisher's advantage. Most traditional books fight very hard to find sufficient market, distribution, and sales, while the coverage given to the book is also negligible. Many printed books may never find a well-known bookstore shelf leave alone a table display. To be a successful author, he or she may need to sell at least 5000-10000 copies and this volume may justify the advance given by the publisher. These reasons may force many new authors to seek the help of self-publishing that usually sells books in all known formats.

Different book publication platforms

It makes a perfect sense to publish your book in both print and ebook. The most significant advantage of publishing by using this approach is that a large number of readers can easily spot the book all over the world, in libraries, bookstores, online libraries, and e-retailers. To see your book sold everywhere, you should find a publishing channel that adopts an expanded distribution approach. Expanded distribution channel means an opportunity to see your book gather a larger readership base through additional numbers of online retailers, bookstores, libraries, institutions and distributors spread around the world.

In addition, you should also be able to see your book published on different ebook selling platforms. Also called hybrid publishing, Penguin-Random House owned Author Solutions, Archway Publishing (Simon & Schuster), Westbow Press (Thomas Nelson), Elite Online Publishing, Balboa Press (Hay House), Abbott Press (Writer's Digest), Hachette owned Perseus Books, She Writes Press, Ingram Wholesale and Ingram Publisher Services are some well-known publishing channels that use both print and ebook distribution services.

Note: Beware of gatekeepers (literary agents) who might insist on you paying them a deep cut out of total book sales. Unfortunately, traditional publishers never accept unsolicited manuscripts and you may need to find an agent to submit your writing samples.

Author Solutions

The Hybrid publishing platform offers the convenience of traditional print as well as ebook formats. There are many group-publishing portals like AuthorHouse, iUniverse, Trafford Publishing, Xlibris, Palibrio, Archway Publishing, Elite Online Publishing, Balboa Press, LifeRich Publishing, Booktango, Alliant Press and 5 More Minutes.

Archway Publishing

According to Archway Publishing goals mentioned on their website, it "promises to help you bring your book to market using an effective combination of self-publishing and traditional methods. By choosing to self-publish with Archway Publishing, you maintain editorial and design control over your book, but benefit from our professional guidance throughout the publishing process."

Westbow Press

This traditional publishing house offers supported self-publishing packages and services for Christian authors. According to the web site's description, "Thomas Nelson & Zondervan, WestBow Press titles will be regularly reviewed by the parent companies and appropriate titles would be chosen for print publication."

Balboa Press

On the Balboa Press about page, it claims that "by choosing Balboa Press as your book publishing company, you not only align yourself with a publisher that shares your values, but you also receive benefits you won't find with any other self-publishing companies." As an author, your book will get a print and ebook edition.

Abbott Press

In its home page, Abbott Press states that... "for years authors have been trying to find a way to publish professional, high-quality books without having to go through a traditional publishing house. Indie publishing, or self-publishing, finally gives authors the freedom to put their books in print." In addition, Abbott Press also states in its website that ... "it combines the best of traditional and self-publishing models to allow you to stay in control of your book publishing process while producing a book that will fill you with pride. Publishing with Abbott Press ensures that your title is accessible to thousands of retailers around the globe, which is critical if you are serious about selling copies of your book. Channel distribution enables your book to be ordered by and distributed to online booksellers and retailers around the world. This allows you to reach a wide audience and compete in the book marketplace."

Perseus Books

Perseus Books is a Hachette Book Group company, consisting of different imprints like Avalon Travel, Basic Books, Da Capo Press, Da Capo Lifelong, PublicAffairs, Running Press, Seal Press, and Westview Press. Perseus publishing partnerships also include Nation Books and Weinstein Books.

Ingram Wholesale

This recognized publishing company specializes in the publication of books – both printed and digital, and in all their different formats. It also helps an author to reach out to millions of readers from all over the world. A traditional publication firm, Ingram has changed its corporate policy to allow Indie and self-authors to publish their books through their sister websites.

Elite Online Publishing

Elite Online Publishing helps busy entrepreneurs, business leaders, and professionals create, publish, and market their book, to build their business and brand. They are passionate about authors sharing their stories knowledge and expertise to help others. They have made all of their authors #1 Bestsellers. They are adamant on all of their authors keep all the rights and royalties from the book. Elite will put your book on Amazon, Nook, iBooks, Google Books and more. They offer social media marketing services and full marketing campaigns and funnels! Elite create's professional book trailer videos submitted to YouTube, Facebook, LinkedIn, and Blogs. They offer book selling websites with lead capture forms. If you want to find out who is buying your books, you need a lead capture bookselling website. With Elite Online Publishing you get a full hybrid self-publishing and marketing company.

To be successful as an author, readers from across the world should discover your book on diverse publication platforms by including ebooks and print editions. Today, new authors can choose either traditional publishers or self-publishing platforms as tools to reach readers. Changing dynamics and shifting scenarios are forcing well-known traditional publishers to offer both print and non-print editions of books to readers. For example, many of them offer ebook download formats on sites like Amazon, Nook, Kobo, and iBooks. If the traditional, print only publication approach does not satisfy you, you can always self-publish your books or hire a hybrid publisher.

6. FOCUSING ONLY ON UP-FRONT COSTS

– GIVING AWAY DOLLARS TO EARN PENNIES

Money flows to the author - Yog's Law

The Publication world is very deceptive and misleading! Those who understand its inner secrets are more likely to do well, while those rookies who do not understand may fail miserably. Many authors commit numerous mistakes and blunders, because of their lack of knowledge about the murky world of publishing. In fact, they usually focus only on paying up-front costs to publish their books at any cost. Focusing only on upfront costs is dangerous and self-inflicting. Simply speaking, you are the owner of your creation and hence the master of the work because of intellectual capital invested in the book. In effect, publishers who want to make money from selling your book should pay you without fail. Obviously, you should protect your asset (i.e., the book) very wisely and in a judicious manner. Likewise, your publication rights and money generated out of any sales are also equally important. Never ever, part of your property so easily. This applies to all forms of publishing, including traditional and self-publishing.

You should identify your goal first in order to single out the most important thing that is dearest to you. Most authors want to make money, name, and fame. If this is the case, you should be aware of circumstances that rob you of the hard-earned money. If it is not the case, then you can negotiate with publisher/agent to decide the amount that you need to pay them in order to publish the book. The second scenario is the most common in academic publishing, where scholarly authors want to publish their books just to highlight it to the academic world; in fact, every such publication enhances their academic credential and standing. However, popular fiction and non-fiction writers want to earn money more than any other thing, especially for personal use.

The ground rule for those who want to make money is that they should visualize the quantum of money they can make from the publishers after selling books. Big and medium-sized publishers usually pay advances and royalties, and they never charge anything to the author before publication. Other publications, who are smaller may never offer fat advances to an author; however, they are more likely to pay higher percentages of royalties to make up for the lack of advances. You might think publishers are expected to cover marketing and promotion costs, but this isn't the case. While bigger houses include marketing costs to a certain extent, smaller and self-publishing companies may not include marketing. Therefore, you should ask for a marketing plan and find out the costs involved. You may need to hire your publisher for marketing and promotion. The same case applies to editors too. If they are working with a publisher, you may need to pay an upfront cost to them for editing or ghostwriter services.

However, you may wish to pay when you hire an outside editor who is either a freelancer or an outsourcing professional. Many publishers use another way to charge you upfront. They may assign someone in the editorial department and ask you to contact them for editorial services. Whatever you do, make sure that you read your contract and do your due diligence before signing.

Understanding the publishing payment system

"New author's novel sells for thousands and lands a big three book series contract! Record advances paid to a new author! New author has a million-dollar book contract!"

You might have already seen industry headlines and media tag-lines screaming about the large sum of money a traditionally published author makes! It is so common to see website promos that highlight massive advances paid to a rookie authors too. With those impressive headlines, a new author will get mesmerized and excited! However, have you ever thought how published traditional authors get their money?

Just consider these surprising factors. You already know the money you spent for your self-published book. You also see the money that you pay for the editor, publisher, cover designer, and marketing department. Once you place your book into the marketplace, you are sure of the amount of money that you would earn in the future, because almost every cent earned out of the sales belongs to you. In many ways, money earned from the self-published book is not termed royalties. Rather, you could call them as your income earned fully and in its entirety. Here, you will never license your book to them, nor will you cede your book rights to anyone. Any advances and royalties payable to an author, are the commercial terms listed in the domain of traditional book publishing industry.

Differences between advance and royalty

Almost all authors often get confused when they hear technical terms like author advances and author royalties. Although both of them sound similar, there are significant differences between them in the manner in which publishers pay them to authors. In the traditional printing world, advances usually mean a sort of loan made to the author without charging any interest. In essence, advances are paid as advances over your future royalties. You will receive this payment, depending on the number of copies that your book will sell in the future, says the first year. There is a standard calculation model to find out the advances that an author will receive before the publication of the book. However, advances are a sort of camouflage payments made to the author, because he or she will have to earn out the advances made. It also means that the author will need to sell a minimum number of copies that it would take to earn the amount of royalties.

However, this earning-out situation may never arise in most of the cases. The only consolation that you can find with this type of payment is that you need not return even a cent of the advance made to you, even if your book fails to sell beyond the "earning out" amount. Once this happens, you can forget approaching the publisher for another book contract. Traditional publishers are very nervous, fickle minded, and they never like to lose in the first place. When an author fails to do well in the market, his or her reputation gradually wears out in the publishing world. You know how whispers about your failed book travel from one publisher's corridor to the other!

Authors may also come across another kind of payment system called "installment plan." Many publishers never give advance to authors in one lump-sum amount. Rather, they will divide the overall payment in smaller chunks and pay each chunk one at a time; typical portion payments start with the signing of the contract, while smaller payments come to the author after writing, editing and post-publication. These smaller payments could be three or four, and at times, could even be five or six. Although it looks very attractive to new authors, the payments made would be very small, because publishers would never pay a bigger advance to a rookie author. Nevertheless, remember that you will never get more money unless you sell a sufficient number of copies that match the royalties earned from your book. In simple words, the advances earned by you should be equal to the advances made before.

Tip: If you are a new author, never expect to earn a very big advance. It would be foolish to think if you think that you can earn thousands from your book! Most mid-list authors usually get $10,000 as advances that too for a set of two or three books written over a period of two or three years. It means that you will lock yourself out for this duration without writing any other books. New authors usually get a meager amount of advances and this may never exceed $5000! Unfortunately, smaller presses never pay you any advances, as they do not have the ability to pay advances to a score of authors at the same time. However, smaller presses usually make for this lacuna by offering better royalty rates. The overall benefit is that you will get regular payments, as and when your books sell in the market.

On the contrary, royalties are the residual and passive type of income that keeps on coming to you as long as your book sells in the market. They would occur regularly in exchange for selling books to a reader who buys them after paying a price. In fact, you will be leasing your book earning an income to a traditional publisher, although you are the intellectual property holder for the book. For the cost production of the book and for introducing it to the market, your publisher pays a certain amount of royalty to you and it is payable at regular intervals. Book royalties might look to be the best thing that happens to you! The saddest part of traditional publishing is that your royalty payments are at best meager and insignificant because you will be ceding many rights to traditional publishers before getting the book to market. This appears to be losing situation to all authors. Almost all publishers have a system of royalty payments that are too cumbersome to comprehend and understand. More often, the royalty rates allotted to authors are pretty smaller.

Would a publisher offer a royalty rate that is worth your honest effort? Honestly, no one is sure what will happen before signing a book contract. The most common royalty rates offered to new authors are 8% for paperback books and 10% for hardbound books at the street price tagged for the market. In the case of a paperback, the average price of the book is about $7.50, while a hardbound book may sell for $20. When you calculate your royalty rate, it seems like a small payment. Sometimes, it may not be even worth your endeavor, considering the overall sales of a book that is usually disappointing for most of the authors. In some cases, a publisher may calculate royalty rates on 50% cover price of the book; the other 50% is allocated for printing and publication costs, plus wholesale and retail margin offered to sellers. In the academic publishing world, this is a common practice. Hence, becoming a self-published author would be a better idea, because the earnings from each sale would be much more. Usually, the production cost of an ebook is fare lesser too. Just think of all those huge amounts of money circulating in the traditional publishing world.

Note: You will need to reach the point where you can start earning royalties beyond the advances given to you. A sliding scale used by a publisher means that after a certain number of sales figure, the author will get an enhanced royalty rate (may be from 8% to 10%). It also means that your book has proven profitable to your publisher. From this point onwards, you are the candidate for a second book contract from the same publisher! Be aware of the royalty report that you receive periodically from the publisher! This report could be very confusing and difficult to understand because it gives a cumulative report of all sales including ebook, hardbound and paperback sales.

In the beginning, a royalty report may show a negative balance against your name because of the money received as an advance payment. Also, remember that the publisher will reserve some amount of money against your name just in case the book fails to sell or when the retailers decide to return unsold copies to the publisher. The amount reserved will continue to adjust as and when there are returns. You may need to go through the statement to understand the secrets of royalty payments. In a majority of cases, an author may end up getting very low payments as royalties apart from those lowly advance payments. Money management can be difficult with traditional publishing.

7. Failure to Become #1

– Failed Opportunity to Become a Celebrity

For an author, the D-Day is the day when the book in the pipeline becomes a reality. He or she will feel content and extremely satisfied when the book is launched online or hits the bookshelves of a bookstore and starts selling like hotcakes. However, even the most cherished dream may turn sour, when the book fails to sell a desired number of copies, and when you or the publisher declares it as a failure! Now, the question is, how the book can become a failure when the content and production quality of the book is above par? Are there any reasons for this possible occurrence? Most obviously, a book will become a commercial failure, when there is no backing from a solid marketing and promotion campaign. The next question is, who will be conducting marketing campaign and promotion? The answer is yes, the publisher is responsible for marketing books. This is true in the case of large traditional publishers. Now, the last question is, do publishers promote and market books? The answer is no, they usually do not promote and market books. Unfortunately, publishers may not take the initiative without an author's active intervention and support. An author's involvement is necessary for publishers to go for a full-fledged marketing campaign.

Marketing strategies for printed books are entirely different from those that are implemented for selling an ebook on an online platform. Therefore, any marketing and promotion technique used should direct and channelize their focused effort towards selling both printed and ebooks in an equal quantity. Many inexperienced authors plan to sell their self-published ebooks on popular online sites, for which the package of marketing strategies varies considerably. Usually, online marketing is extremely dynamic and its techniques keep changing every day. It is important to have a marketing plan for the launch of the ebook as well as a plan for the launch of the print book. If you have a marketing plan and roadmap and the right marketing team you can reach a bestseller status on Amazon or New York Times.

Amazon bestseller is a reachable target and some hybrid publishers offer this service. The campaign may include lowering the price of the ebook to .99 cents. It may also include a book landing page that gives your book away with the customer paying shipping fees only. Many bestsellers like Tony Robbins, Brendon Bouchard, and Jeff Walkers have used this model. Make sure you have a plan to become a bestseller. This title will help you create instant credibility and expert status. You will not only be an author, you will be a bestselling author. When implementing a marketing plan, make sure your aim is for a bestselling book!

What do publishers do when your book is ready for marketing?

Marketing and book promotion is possible in many different ways. The publisher or your hybrid publishing company may promote it by using different methods. The extent of book promotion, marketing, and selling sometimes depends directly on the author's reputation as a "profitable author." If you are a new author, a traditional publishing may not promote your book with all these methods. Your publisher or hybrid publishing company can promote and market your book in the following ways:

- Placing your book in catalogs for distribution to online portals, offline bookstores, retailers, wholesalers, libraries, and trade exhibition
- Provide promotional materials to the sales team, who in turn approach different channels and promote the book in a big way
- Place brochures on online bookstores, advertisement channels, and other platforms, through which a reader will come to know that your book ready for sale
- Sending out advance copies to reviewers, critics, and commentators
- Sending free promotional copies to select online readers
- Publishing press releases in online and offline magazines
- Dispatching books for exhibition in book fairs and conventions
- Promoting book on Amazon exclusively, because a large numbers

of reads congregate on this site

- Social media promotion by using various channels like Twitter, Facebook, Instagram, StumbleUpon and others
- Online blog tour and interview on well-known websites
- Offline tour on talk shows, book signing groups, lecture circuits and press interview
- Possible TV talk shows and podcast interviews

However, there is a big caveat here! These exercises are possible with traditional publishers only with your active participation and cooperation. Book publishers are known to promote and market those authors, who are ready to provide a ready-made list of readers, reader groups, blog writers and social media influences! In other words, your role is as important as the role that is played by publishers. Although traditional publishers never announce it explicitly, they always give out a hint that the authors' responsibility also counts for ensuring the success of a book in the market. If you want to access all features of a full marketing and promotional campaign, you may need to consider the self-publishing or hybrid publishing route that includes your full marketing plan or roadmap.

Here are some reasons why many traditional publishers hesitate to market your book:

- The publisher that you chose may not have enough money, time or staff to promote your book.

- The publisher may not have the contacts or resources to reach your target readership. In fact, such publishers should be avoided at any cost.

- They may not know different ways of using resources that are required for marketing in an appropriate manner; they may lack the metrics or qualifiers to measure their marketing efforts.

- Publishers can place your books almost immediately in major bookstores, retail shops, and online portals. Indeed, they excel in distribution and dispatching. Nevertheless, just placing books in the appropriate places is not enough. Readers should be able to find, retrieve, and buy it to ensure a confirmed sale to the author. A book will never reach its intended audience by itself! Someone has to lead and guide a reader to the book so that a purchase decision can be made.

- Another important reason for rejection is an author's lack of presence in the publishing market. Authors who have many published works in their name are more likely to get marketing preference over those who are first-timers. Similarly, publishers are known to put more efforts on those book contracts that received a higher advance. A new author may find sourcing proper marketing support very difficult and tedious.

- Publishers tend to disregard or ignore authors who do not have a considerable social media presence. They also need a list of readers with whom they can establish contacts directly.

- Authors, who lack a large targeted email list, may not get enough attention from publishers.

- Many publishers would love those authors who are ready to sign an agreement for profit sharing deals. This is also known as a "black loaded book deal", is this acceptable by authors? Authors who do not agree to sign this deal may be ignored by publishers.

- Publishers usually sign deals with authors, whose books can tap the full market across different geographical localities.

According to Mike Shatzkin, the Founder & CEO of The Idea Logical Company, *"the biggest shortcoming of traditional publishers these days is their failure to help authors help themselves with digital marketing."* In his address at Digital Book World, he also stated, *"every house should do a "digital audit" for every author they sign that includes concrete suggestions for filling in gaps and improving discoverability and engagement. To my knowledge, not one of them does."* Dissecting his opinions would reveal several hidden secrets because an author is always short-changed by traditional publishers be it in marketing promotion or in paying correct royalty rates. Today's publishing world invariably depends on the internet technology and its applications. Those who are expert in creating a solid web presence are more likely to succeed in selling more numbers of books. Though many authors are very good writers, not all authors are technical-savvy and don't know much about reaching out to online readers or prospective buyers. The first and foremost important issue is whether an author can fast learn how to set up a website or a blog site to reach out to hundreds of probable buyers.

While it is true that all authors are required to create their web presence, a publisher's non-cooperation in helping authors to set up an efficient web page can never be pardoned. Most publishers believe that they are very much in tune with an author's web presence and that they can readily tap available online contacts to reach readers on behalf of the author. However, this effort can only complement an author's digital footprint. They just cannot rely only on the author's web presence. In other words, they may need to do more to help authors to market their books in large numbers. In this regard, landing pages are very critical for book success. Both the author and publisher will need to set up a set of landing pages that compliment the effort, money and time invested by them. Hence, authors will need to be very careful, while choosing a publisher, because author alone cannot ensure the full success of the book. One cannot expect publishers and editors to be very proficient in digital marketing. Similarly, authors cannot become digital marketing masters overnight.

Both of them will need to understand the important roles of websites and social media presence in the marketing effort. Again, the author should be very careful in selecting a publishers marketing ability and support extended, especially in terms of digital marketing. Most hybrid publishers and marketing companies possess the required resources (both monetary and labor) to set up a full-fledged digital marketing campaign. In the process, they should help collaborating authors gain a foothold in the fiercely competitive publishing world. If they cannot ensure this help, authors may need to look elsewhere for help or seek the digital help of those who can provide one instantly. In today's cutthroat publishing business, you may need to equip yourself with some minimum digital technical know-how. In excepting self-publishing almost all traditional publishers frequently demand an author's considerable digital presence.

A traditional publisher may audit an author's ability to provide the following:

- A fully functional author website that highlights details about the author, his or her work, book details and a brief biography
- Comprehensive author and book information published on sites like Goodreads and LibraryThing. The author's presence on Amazon works to an author's advantage
- Google+ presence and connection to check author's social media reach
- A complete social media presence on sites like Twitter, Facebook, StumbleUpon and Pinterest, LinkedIn, Instagram and more.
- Email opt-in lists
- Message Board and Forum participants and their email addresses
- Cross-promotional efforts

Note: Every author needs his or her digital presence and a formidable web portal that highlights achievements and details about author's life. Presumably, an author should put some real-time efforts to promote books sales and enhance author status. However, one cannot expect an author to take full control of book marketing and promotion because of lack of funds, effort, time or resources. Publishers should be an equal partner in progress and they should ensure maximum help and assistance to new authors so that their work is also given equal importance that is usually accorded to top end authors. Consider self-publishing or choose a hybrid publisher and marketing team that will provide the digital marketing needed to have a successful book.

Publicity marketing leads to enhanced book footprint

In a nutshell, publicity marketing is targeting the media to distribute the details of your published book. You will need to reach as many media sources as possible with a clear and loud message that people should read your book and find benefits from it. People from all over the world should access details about your book and its content. To achieve this goal, you or your publisher must set up a press release campaign to create media hype, book pitch, and exposure.

Internet technology-enabled marketing and promotion

The digital world is the ultimate truth today. Without the internet, none can survive. A book can survive only with a focused and balanced, internet-based marketing campaign. It is an invaluable tool to reach out to prospective readers in a big way. The internet network can help you go global from your present local status. It can help you reach both national and international markets with the least amount of effort. Your publisher or marketing team should help you reach out to thousands of readers on social media platforms like Facebook and Instagram. Twitter is another great tool, sending out real-time and live feedback on your book. Google's search engine marketing and StumbleUpon's Paid Discovery services are an excellent way to create awareness about your book. In addition, publishers should also help you with website design services, so that readers can visit the site by clicking on the landing page created on publisher web portals. Google Display Network helps you run an advertisement exercise on your book to reach over 2 million Google partner websites. Barnes and Noble, GoodReads, and Amazon Search are some of the most famous search services that readers can use to find your book. You should also promote your book on at least 25 well-known publishing and book blog and this exercise will help spread messages about your upcoming book.

Kirkus Book Sampling Services is yet another online source, where publishers can post messages about the book and its content. Some publishers provide a Publishers Weekly Online Bundle to new authors. This allows you to extend your online reach by posting positive messages about your book. Your publisher or marketing team must also provide free sample chapters to its site visitors; this helps you catch the attention of potential book buyers. GoodReads is perhaps the largest online community of book readers. You may wish to list your book in this review portal to help readers grade and review the book.

Online video advertising is both vocal as well as visual

Videos are some of the most effective tools for marketing and promotion. When used appropriately, this tool can be the potential platform that provides both visual and vocal messages to target intended audience. It is extremely dynamic and entertaining too! Book video marketing services are mandatory for the success of your book. Today's readers want action-oriented video content before buying a book. It also helps you create an author brand. Your video should explain the finer details of your book to prospective readers. A personal message from the author can kick start book marketing and promotion in a forceful manner. YouTube is a popular video sharing platform. Video marketing can help first-time authors to reach out to thousands of viewers by using different channels. In fact, YouTube videos can captivate and target specific audiences in an effective way. Consider adding your videos to Channels like YouTube, Vimeo, Dailymotion, and Facebook.

Send printed materials to a target audience and get connections

Printed marketing and promotional materials are perhaps the oldest tools that helped a traditional publisher to reach out to potential book buyers. If you want to have a highly effective book marketing campaign, you must use printed materials; in fact, they are the foundation for all successful book marketing campaigns. Book signing events and media reach-out exercises would need a large number of printed materials, brochures, and flyers. Your publisher or marketing team should provide beautifully designed flyers and brochures to all bookstores, both online and offline so that they catch the attention and interest of a book reader. An author should also get a fully supplied marketing starter kit that can be used to promote the book. A personal bundle will help you fine-tune the actual book campaign in your area of activity. New York Review of Books promotion, Readers Digest marketing reach out, Publisher's Weekly inserts, NY Times Sunday Book Review, INGRAM Catalog Marketing, Ingram Supplement Marketing are some of the best instruments available to push the book through to thousands of readers. Some of these platforms boast of millions of subscribed readers and their immense reach is universal and far-reaching; for example, New York Times Sunday Book Review readership is more than a million, while Reader's Digest is the most loved magazine in the world.

Book Reviews by reputable reviewers can enhance your sales

Book reviews, in an appropriate form, would provide a real picture of the book and its contents. A book's impact or influence on readers is far more effective when someone publishes an in-depth review in a well-known magazine or online journal. Your publisher or marketing team should be able to seek the help of noted book reviewers to create a detailed review of the book. All positive reviews will help your book successfully make a recognizable brand and create a strong sales pitch. For example, BlueInk Review publishes reviews of self-published books. In addition, Trifecta Review Service would provide three different reviews of the same book that can fruitfully enhance the reputation and buy-ability.

AudioBooks – Innovative Tools to captivate reader's attention

Audiobooks are the current craze among reading population. It is also neat, non-aging and highly effective. A book in its audio form will help readers understand the main story, its plot and eventually feel the ultimate emotion in the reading process. In other words, an audio CD involves a human talking to another human with active and forceful storytelling. All publishers should supply and publish audio books as a mandatory requirement. In fact, it is mandatory and essential. An author should also ask the publisher to release audio CDs of books published. Let there be a link to an audiobook on the purchase page. As of 2017 audioBooks are the fastest growing segment in the publishing industry, with over $2.5 billion in sales. This number will continue to grow. The best marketing agencies and publishers will offer audiobooks, CDs, professional voiceover and publication.

Radio and TV advertising – Mass communicating ideas to reach millions

Both podcast or radio and TV advertising are the most commonly used promotional tools. They are traditional, yet very powerful. Ask your publisher or marketing team to include podcast or radio and TV marketing and promotion in the contract form. Most publishers can arrange radio and TV interviews with authors. Be an advertising manager yourself and spread the message about your book in a forceful manner.

Book marketing and promotion is a tedious job. Authors just cannot do it alone and need active help from the hybrid publisher or book marketing team. Before signing a book contract, an author should insist on a full marketing and promotional package that includes everything mentioned above. In many cases, the publisher may refuse to sign the contract and they may even want you to commit to a self-generated marketing plan. In the meantime, please remember that you alone as a writer cannot ensure the success of the book. Invariably, you will need the help and assistance from your publisher or marketing team. So reject any publisher who refuses to market and promote your book. Look beyond such publishers and find the one who can provide you with the full package. Hybrid publishers that help you self-publish will include marketing and promotional packages. Make sure you have a marketing team to help get your book off the ground.

8. Not Having an Online Author Presence

– Lost Identity in the Digital World

Are you an established author with many books to your credit? If you are, then you can expect readers contacting retailers to buy books. Not all writers are professionals and well identified in the author circuit. Thousands of them are trying to publish their first book and they may not know the tricks of publishing books and marketing them later to readers buy them. The book publishing industry is slowly migrating to a digital environment. This shifting scenario applies to traditional publishers too, who used to market only printed book until recently. In order to survive in the industry, authors will need to learn and master digital marketing strategies and methods. Unfortunately, for those who want to succeed in the publishing world, the digital world is highly saturated and it is almost impossible for authors to gain readers' attention within the shortest possible time. In a digital world, where publishers are very reluctant to spend their dollars on extended marketing and promotions of books, new authors will need to find a way to compete with fortunate ones who are already ahead on the path to success.

Nevertheless, new authors can succeed with a little bit of proper planning and execution of thoughtful digital ideas. They might easily challenge the monopoly of well-known publishers, who try to bulldoze authors with their preposterous clauses and rules that are at the most stifling and gut-wrenching. It is easy to reach the top if you know how you can market and promote your book digitally and virtually. Not having an online author presence is a great mistake, as almost all authors are known to promote their book online. In fact, reaching readers through the traditional means is an old idea. If you do not have a firm digital footprint, your book may never sell in the market, because more than 75% of book sale is closed digitally and in the wide world of web. Internet marketing is highly competitive, especially for printed and ebooks. Still, you can make it to the top by applying latest and practical internet marketing strategies. Here are some of the essential steps that you will need to follow in order to market and promote your book in the highly aggressive internet domain.

Amazon Author Page

If you have a book on Amazon, you need to claim your Amazon author page. Amazon is loved by search engines like Google, Yahoo/ Bing and more. If you have not claimed your Amazon author page you need to. Simply go to Amazon Author Central. Claim your page with a custom URL like; http://www.amazon.com/author/jennfoster.

Claim your book and optimize your Amazon author page with:

- Pictures
- Videos
- Full Author Bio with Links to:
    - Social Media
    - Website
    - Digital training products
    - Anywhere else you want the reader to go
- Blog RSS feed
- Events

With an Amazon Author page, you will rank high on Google and other search engines when people are looking for you. This alone gives you the credibility and expert status you need to close more business.

Author website is a primary requirement

An author website is a focused area of activity that helps you propagate your ideas, expression, and intellect to your audience. It also helps you introduce the work you did as an author. An author website can provide a wonderful pitch to your book too. In addition, it is a great online business card. The principal benefits of having a website are as follows:

- It tells who you are
- It announces what you do
- It provides a background for your book
- It also gives you information about your previous book
- It opens up your social media channel so that readers can interact with you
- It is a broadcasting tool that helps readers talk about your book
- It is also a selling place for your book
- It also demonstrates that you are a true professional, who can interact with readers in a friendly and skilled approach

Note: At first, setting up your online presence may look a daunting task. However, it is not that complicated to design and create an author website. If your publisher does not help you with your website, you will have to act quickly to launch your website, because marketing and promotion of your book start at least three months before the release of the book.

How to run a free website to market your book

Creating a new website is quite easy. It is not too expensive either. You can design your website by using one of these two approaches: free to use platforms and paid options. Apart from WordPress and Blogger (BlogSpot), not all other free to use websites are desirable for book marketing and promotion, because they may not give you an individual online identity.

For example, If you choose WordPress free hosting, your name of the website would be www.yourname.wordpress.com, where "yourname" is the exact spelling and author name. Similarly, on choosing BlogSpot or Blogger, your website name would be www.yourname.blogspot.com.

WordPress and Blogger are two of the recognized online blog platforms that one can use for creating an author website. Both of them provide you with regular updates, user-oriented add-on, plugin, hundreds of colorful and feature-rich themes and great security features. Above all, you can even develop a website with minimum technical know-how without consulting expensive design developers. The main drawbacks of using free blogging websites are:

- Customization of the site to match your needs and preferences is limited
- Limited functionality could put you in trouble, especially if you are planning for a shopping cart on the site to sell the book

- You may not be able to get advanced details about readers and their personal preferences
- Difficult to install sophisticated, paid plugin and widgets that can help you utilize full features of a website

If you are an unpublished author, free hosting via WordPress and Blogger makes good sense, because you are on the road to developing an author brand in your name; in fact, it will be your first digital journey. Migrating from free WordPress to paid version is also a good idea because it is perhaps one of the easiest platforms to manage a website with most of the features readily available to you.

There are a few other free website builder options online that work wonders for the average person. Wix, Squarespace, and Weebly are all great options for building a website quickly and easily. If you are tech savvy you can build it yourself or consider hiring a Wix Professional. Search your local Google Maps for a web designer in your hometown. It isn't very expensive to have a local web designer create a masterpiece author website for you to sell your book and brand you as an Author, Expert, and Public Figure.

Paid options or fee-based hosting is a self-hosted form of web hosting

The cost of owning a fee-based web hosting may range from a few dollars per month to hundreds or even thousands. Options that are more expensive are outside the WordPress platform and they are very pricey to maintain and manage. Almost all authors use this option to create and establish their author brands. Self-hosting provides you full control over your website and gives full access to your website, its files and hosting platforms; in other words, you can tweak your website and its features in any way you want, and assume full responsibility to your action and choices. The main advantages of self-hosting include:

- Full customizability of the website, its design, features, files, folders, templates, plugins, and widgets
- Offers a long-term planning for establishing an author brand
- Provides a deep insight into the web traffic, its geo-location, e-commerce performance metrics and other vital parameters that would allow you to further tweak the website performance for best results
- An opportunity to add additional functionality to enhance the practicality of website
- An option that allows you gather user database, their opinions, expressions, and choices
- Create a big list of readers, who can potentially buy the book
- Gather email lists through opt-in registration; this approach will help you send a periodic update and additional information about your website, newsletters, forthcoming books and an in-depth detail about the current book that you are promoting

Designing a website

You are your own, self-made architect for the website. You can design a website based on existing needs, requirements and most of the websites try to match visitors' on-site preferences. However, you will need to include right type of web pages in your website. Some of the most common web pages are:

Homepage: This page acts as a window through which you can reach the publishing world. On this page, you will display details about the book, its content in a nutshell and various other social media icons that helps you create a long list of reader subscribers. When visitors land on your site, they should be able to read the content provided on the landing page. Include detailed information on the book and tell why your book is important in its genre. Include a tagline and eye-catching profile of the book along with its colorful cover. You may also need to summarize how the book can provide innumerable benefits your reader.

Personal profile page: This page enlightens the readers more about you and your achievements. Be kind and warm to the visitor who visits the site. Be a true professional and include personal information on details like how you entered the world of writing books and why this profession was important to you. Always use a third person language because this kind of narrative is straightforward and readers always like this simple approach. Let the profile be short, crisp because readers are very fickle minded, and they may not like to spend more time on any web page unless some details capture their attention and appeal them to remain on the page.

Book page: Include a blurb for books you wrote in your life. Include links to reach those books, so that readers can navigate to the pages where you listed them. Also, include hyperlinks to various online stores where readers are can purchase books. Again, the main objective of this page is to cajole and compel readers to read, understand, spread messages about published books and buy them in the process.

An author blog: The most important tool in the digital publishing world is an author blog. On this page, you can write articles, critiques, short memoirs and other snippets on anything that is connected to the world of books and publishing. You can invite readers to post comments and opinions. Ensure that you reply each one of them without fail. Best authors of the day write some of the most interesting blogs. Most blogs written by author bloggers share two important attributes: they are fresh and are extremely interesting.

A blog connects you and the book to your readership. An appropriately designed blog can establish you as a subject expert, which eventually helps you bag future projects and speaking engagements. To be a successful blogger, you will need to write and publish authentic content that carries only useful reader-centric information. You can share whatever you want with your readers and seek replies from them. With each successful blogging day, you can see email list growing bigger in length.

Contact page: A contact page is very important part of a website because it acts as an active conduit between you and the readers. It also lets readers contact you by using the contact information provided by you. The contact page should include your e-mail address, social media links and a website contact form that would permit readers to contact you directly. On this page, you can also include Cookies and Privacy

Policy links to let readers know important legal details about your site and readers' roles and responsibilities.

Building a lasting web presence

Possibly, the most effective and affordable way to reach readers is by putting together a very strong web presence. Nothing can be more valuable than using social media links and posting real-time messages across to thousands of readers. You can never ignore social media as a tool of today's digital marketing. It is a new way of building a list of dedicated followers.

The main objectives of creating social media contacts and posting great content are to build trust and loyalty. Another important goal is to connect with your reader, both emotionally and practically; this approach leads to increased sales volume, as well as better interaction and meaningful dialogs between you and the reader.

Secrets of a successful social media campaigner

Listening to others helps you become a very good sales strategist. You will need to be a good listener to keep your fans engaged and active. When you are a good listener, you will start knowing and understanding more about readers, their preferences, interests, liking and different issues they like and follow. In other words, a successful social media campaign has two main phases: understanding the audience and comprehending issues they are currently talking right now. The best strategy is to post relevant and meaningful content that takes care of interests of both parties: you and the readers. The whole issue with social media posting is not about you or your interests. In fact, you have to give your fans something that they really need and want. In other words, you will have to provide a humane touch to your postings, so that readers understand why they should read you, your book and postings. When the postings are emotional and appealing, readers will start listening to you, which is a process that usually terminates in an increased sales volume.

Already, we know that numerous issues drive and create social connections. The psychology of social media is very difficult to understand and comprehend. Firms and companies spend a lot of money and time to find out those motivational factors that drive clients to buy products and services. You can easily boost your online presence by reading free reports that highlight and explain reasons that generally drive clients to buy a specific product or service. To get a deeper inspiration and to read latest research survey reports on social media, you can visit sites like Pew Internet, Social Times, Statista Buffer, Marketo, and Nielsen.

Follow these checklists to build your list of readers, who can potentially buy your book in the future:

Post text with relevant images: All images posted on blogs are the heart and soul of social media postings. They can instantly attract, cajole, and compel a reader to read embedded messages. In fact, a "stop-check-read" tool, it allows readers to read blog messages and reply their answers in return. Nevertheless, the images and illustrations posted on all posts should match the content and its inner meaning.

Posts that gather comments from readers: All postings on social media should successfully elicit comments and critiques from readers. As an author, you should give something that allows them to talk and open their minds. Let your postings be a catalyst to start a conversation. Also, allow readers post their replies and seek answers from you in return. Make sure that the discussion channel is always open to all readers.

All posts should lead to book promotion: All your postings should contain intelligently placed textual links that lead to book buy page, where readers can make a decision to buy the book or not. Nonetheless, this promotion should never be direct and appealing. In other words, you should never ask readers to buy the book directly. Rather, you can use links embedded within the post that is contextual to the published book.

Link postings: Any blog article posted should read like a story or anecdote. Provide readers a chance to think about the post and take action based on informed decisions. Insert links intermittently within the postings. If a reader shows an interest, she or he will click on the link to navigate straight to the book title page where additional information on the book is readily available.

Suggest and advise readers when they are in doubt: All readers need help, assistance, and guidance from you. Social media is a sort of compendium of useful information. If readers want some help and assistance, you should be able to give them instantly. This simple approach will lead to an immediate emotional bonding between you and the reader. People simply love straightforward answers and solutions.

People need discounts, giveaways, and rebates: Not too greedy, people usually want something from you in the form of a reward or freebie. Most of the time, they may need a free sample chapter from the book or an ebook download about a specific topic. Countless fresh authors want professional advice in the form of newsletters and ebooks. You may want to provide them free ebooks, sample chapters, and newsletters at regular intervals.

People need constant encouragement and inspiration: More or less all people need someone who can motivate, catalyze and encourage them to achieve something tangible in life. You can act as a mentor, guide, leader or a capable motivator to help them achieve their goals and realize cherished dreams. They are just like you, and they might have faced trouble, pain, anger, frustration, and hardships in their life. Moreover, they usually find their comfort and solace in a blog where they can find practical solutions offered by other readers.

Every post on social media should call for an action. Make sure that you allow your fans to take a concrete action. It could be a simple reply or an assured action leading to a confirmed sale.

You can build a successful online presence if you connect people with the following goals in mind:

- Make readers happy and satisfied
- They should feel inspired and rejuvenated
- Be a compassionate listener, who can listen to people
- Provide relevant and practical information
- Be supportive and helping
- Help them connect with you and other helpful resources

Note: The main goal of posting messages is to gather additional readers apart from the regular ones. This will decide whether your posting is a failure or not. An engagement rate is the "overall number of readers who take action vs. total numbers of readers who subscribed to your blog", and this can be in either in percentage or in numbers. Obviously, we also need more people to click, like and comment on any article or posting. Better connection, trust and loyalty and good content are the three magical potions that act together to create eventual sales. If you do not follow these basic axioms of social media, then a majority of visitors will never return to your website, and even if they do, they may not see the page for more than a few seconds. Make sure that you retain your site visitors by engaging them to stay on it.

The world of digital marketing is dynamic and fast changing. You may need to be readily adaptable to any changes in the digital ambiance. It is difficult to assess and evaluate the mood of digital assets. Just consider using the legendary Pareto's Time Management rule: Spend your time on those things that actually give results to you. Dedicate your efforts towards 20% (out of 100%) of the time to attempt doing new things. Similarly, this rule also works for people who can take a definite action to buy your book. Out of 100 people, only 5 or 10 will eventually buy the book and rest will be either readers or they will be those who are postponing the decision to purchase the book.

Building a large mailing list: Social media is a level playing field. It is beneficial to both parties: you and your readers. If you carry out a plan in an appropriate manner, you can build a long list of readers who are ready to receive your newsletters in their inbox. You can also use the opt-in email plug-in on your website to permit readers to register free downloads and newsletters. You can do it alone or you can outsource the service to some of the famous, fee-based consultants like MailChimp, Aweber, iContact, Benchmark Email and Constant Contact. Once you use these external resources, you may try to evaluate and analyze the user data based on their preferences, interests, geographical locations and reading choices. These primary datasets will assist you to dispatch highly targeted messages to promote all future projects and forthcoming books.

Targeting messages to a wider reach of an audience: You can participate in forums, blogs and web portals other than your own in order to promote your book. You may also seek permission from them to post guest content. It is possible for this opportunity to capture future readers to your website. There are hundreds of good book reviews and literary sites and you may choose the best ones to post your messages. Some of the examples are GoodReads, LibraryThing, Addicted to ebooks and Writers Digest. If you are ready to spend some money, you can seek services from external portals to promote your book. These may include Twitter, Facebook advertisements,

GoodReads Ads and Google AdWords. Most of your readers live in various social media platforms like Twitter, Facebook, Instagram, StumbleUpon, GoodReads, LinkedIn, and Pinterest.

GoodReads is sort of Question and Answer tool. Here, the authors will answer reader-generated questions. Many people, who ask questions, will be dedicated fans or new readers who are likely to become future buyers. In Facebook, you will post to your wall and seek answers and comments from your readers. Most authors set up a Facebook page, where readers subscribe and participate in group-interactions. Pinterest is for those authors, who want to publish images of their book pages. Similarly, Instagram is also a picture message board, where you can post your thoughts in a pictorial and thematic format. You might also publish short articles on LinkedIn share pages, while Wattpad allows you to generate free content pages that readers can download, read and comment. Twitter is perhaps the most effective web platform that lets people post messages in short and cryptic form. Twitter re-tweets are the most efficient forms of marketing. In addition, you may buy paid advertisement packs in the above-mentioned sites to promote and market your website, as well as the book.

Nearly all traditional publishers fail to offer the luxury of marketing and promotion in their entirety. This is also true in the case of providing online marketing facilities. Of late, traditional publishers are trying hard to keep pace with the ever-changing dynamics of publishing. New emerging trends like digital publishing, self-publishing, digital marketing, and promotion are forcing traditional publishers to change their business approach. While managing expenses and cost-cutting are the main drivers that restrict a publisher's digital expansion drive, a perceived reluctance to promote new authors is making things more difficult; cost reduction management is explicit in areas like advance payment, marketing, and promotion. As digital promotion is very risky and cumbersome, a publisher may not show keenness towards promoting every author that is accepted for publication. Established authors and those who are more likely to sell books in large quantities are the ones who get preferential treatment. Therefore, first-time authors are usually recommended to get their marketing promotion engine running with their own effort without expecting to get help from their publishers.

9. Self-Publishing

– Gateway to Author Stardom

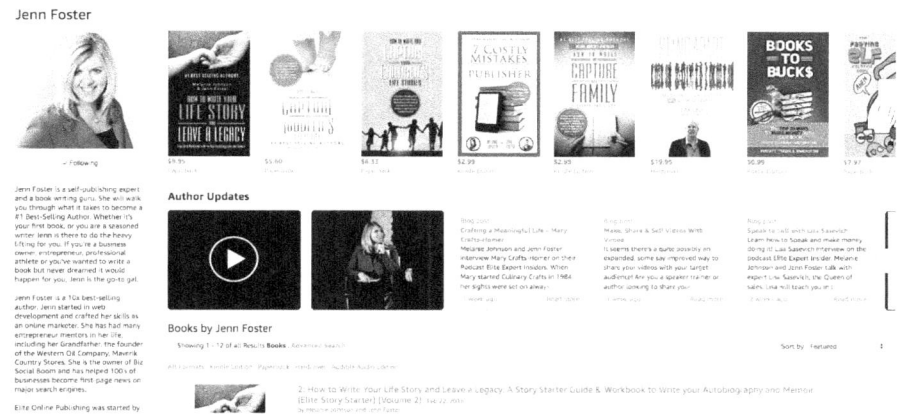

Jenn Foster

Self-publishing is a captivating word. It captures the imagination of thousands of new and first-time authors with the lure of name, fame and book publication success. Earlier, many of them never had a chance to publish their book with a traditional publisher. The odds of getting a published book were minimal, because of very high rejection rates by the publishers. Furthermore, book authors were forced to submit their manuscripts with the help of an agent, who used charge an exorbitant sum of money payable after the book release (percentages varied from 15% to 25%). In addition, publishers were reluctant to help and assist rookie authors with an efficient book-marketing and promotion plan; this was the sole rights of a select few authors, who already established their publishing credibility previously.

New authors were viewed with skepticism and doubt because publishers were never sure of the future commercial success of the book.

If an author wanted to publish a book, he or she had to choose one of those vanity presses, who exploited the writer by snatching away book rights, apart from charging ridiculous upfront fees and hidden fees. However, events started changing during the late 1990s, when print-on-demand (POD) publishers started interacting with new authors. POD means printing books one at a time and sending it to buyers. Publishers offered low cost, publishing packages, because of advantages like non-existent print runs, the absence of book warehousing and inventory keeping. The only major expense involved was money spent on designing the book in terms of manuscript editing, cover graphics art, page setting and overall designing. However, authors failed to sell a decent number of copies of published books, because publishers were keen on selling only online and they never solicited the professional help of booksellers to sell books in bookstores.

By 2010, a remarkable transformation was witnessed in the publishing world, when self-published authors started publishing their ebooks with active help from the largest online retailer, Amazon. Without paying a single cent of an up-front fee, any author can publish and market their ebooks on Amazon. Now, you can publish your ebook in various formats and in different portals like Nook, Kindle, CreateSpace, and iTunes.

Scores of authors hate to publish books with a traditional publisher, because of many reasons like:

- Difficulty in finding a commercial publisher
- Almost all traditional publishers search for an author who can bear the expenses of marketing and promotion
- Most publishers want the author to cede away all forms of book rights
- Loss of book production control in terms of design, manuscript editing revisions and changes in the tone and tenor of the content
- Apparent neglect on part of the publishers, once they publish the book, especially long waiting period for publication
- Very low royalty rates and advance fees
- Very low budget reserved for book marketing and promotion

Conversely, many authors love to self-publish their books, because of convenient advantages that come along with it. Some of these benefits are as follows:

- They retain full control over the book in terms of its content, design, and marketing
- Full author rights over the book manuscript and the published book
- Full retention of revenues earned from the sales of the book
- Maximum royalty earnings from sales of the book (up to 80%)
- Full exploitation of unknown markets that lie in niche areas, as well as in overseas countries
- Increased chances of re-publication into printed book form

- A large, future fan-following, if the author taps the existing social media in a proper manner

Like in traditional publishing, even self-publishing has its share of challenges of which some are listed below:

- Printed self-publishing is still very expensive. Print self-publishers charge a heavy amount to publish books. You may need to spend at least $25,000 to get your book in the print form
- Self-publishing involves an investment of time, money and effort. The time that you invest in it may eventually decide the success or otherwise of the publication
- You will need to spend money on advertising, marketing and promotion of the book. If you overshoot your budget, you may end in incurring heavy losses
- Self-publishing is an individual effort. You are the sole owner of your effort and you may not expect help and assistance from others unless you choose a publisher who publishes books in print form.

Ways to self-publish – Publishing without hassles

You can use three different ways of self-publishing in today's market:

Self-publish on your own: Here, you are the sole traveler in the quest for publishing excellence and you will take the complete responsibility for your actions. In other words, you cannot blame anyone else but you when something goes wrong. In this approach, you will be editing your book and work in tandem with retailers and distributors to sell the book. As this is a solo exercise, you may also need to put a lot effort to publish your book.

Self-publish by seeking the help of a service company who works as your publisher: You will buy different service packages at varying rates from a service partner and get publishing arrangements in return. You may also get services by paying for a customized rate package. A good publishing firm will charge an upfront fee, allow you to retain full book rights and retain 100% sales for yourself. The most common services provided are proofreading, advanced editorial, designing, marketing, and promotion. They will not charge anything on copies of books that you sell. Unfortunately, the publisher will never stock your book in a physical store. If you are ready to pay a substantial amount of up-front fee, you will get an all-inclusive package including an extended marketing plan. In fact, the service offered by some publisher is similar to the one that is offered by a traditional publisher. Another advantage is bypassing intricate regulations of traditional book publishing. Some of the known assisted book publication services are Matador, Mill City Press, Radius Book Group, Book in a Box, CreateSpace and others.

Self-publish with the help of a hybrid company:

Most of the so-called self-publishing services that name themselves as "hybrid publishers" are far-fetched and fanciful, and of the most opaque with their business approach. Any fees charged by them could be very prohibitive, while service standard offered to authors is of poor quality. Before publishing with them, you may need to evaluate their service quality and commercial viability. As an author, you will earn enhanced royalties than the one that is given by a traditional publisher, but far lesser than the one that you receive through self-publishing.

Although self-publishing and subsidy publishing sound similar, there are some subtle differences between them. For example, subsidy publishing means a form of publication where an author will pay an upfront fee to publish a book. On the contrary, self-publishing is a mode of publishing, in which the author will transform himself or herself into a publisher of the book.

Major differences between self-publishing and subsidy publishing

There are major differences between subsidy and self-publishing. Here are some of those differences:

Control over process: With self-publishing, you will retain full control over the entire publication process like writing, proofreading, editing, graphics, images, cover art, and marketing. In contrast, you will get standard, boiler type templates for design, graphics, cover art and other usual paraphernalia. To change these highly customized utilities, you will need to pay the extra money and it will balloon your overall expenditure.

Revenue sharing: Self-publishing allows you to set your own rates and book offer terms. You will also get all possible types of revenues. In the case of subsidy publishing, the publisher will pay a certain percentage of money on overall sales in the form of a royalty.

However, royalty payment could differ based on the quantum of discounts offered and numbers of books sold. Usually, the publisher will set the price of the book and you will have to agree to this condition laid out by the publisher.

Different rights distribution: In the case of self-publishing, the author will own the full book rights. However, if you want to convert a self-published book into a printed one, the publisher will term the book as "previously published." On the contrary, many subsidy publisher demand authors handing over the limited grant of rights, although some of them may ask for full rights.

Ownership of the book: When you self-publish your book, you will own the book in its full avatar. You can do anything you want; change its content, cover, graphics, images and anything that wants changes! In the case of subsidy publishing, you never own the rights to your own book. You will not earn any royalties when you buy your own books! You may purchase the book at an author's discount of 30-40%. It means that you will not get any royalty, but still end up paying for the book at a cost.

Self-publishing – A Basic Primer

To achieve success in publishing, you will need to write and market books that actually sell in the market domain. If you are publishing a book by using the traditional channel, your chances of success depend entirely on the genre that you use to write that book. Non-fiction books are the most suitable for self-publishing. If you know your nonfiction reader group, you can easily write a book to target it. Similarly, if you are an expert in a special area of interest, you can publish a book on that specific domain. To succeed in self-publishing adventure, you will need to create a product that has a "pre-assigned" market or readership. Children' book, a collection of poems and short stories may not sell well in the self-published market, because children's book readers love to glance through printed books before buying them. Similarly, poetry and short stories have a limited readership base. Whatever the case, self-published books still have a lower appeal and success rate.

Most readers and commentators consider self-publishing to be exclusive to writers, who cannot publish their books in a more traditional way. Nonetheless, the trend is slowly changing in the recent past, as more readers are switching over to e-reading devices to read a book. Most self-published books are downloadable as an ebook. It is easy to carry and read anywhere you want. In addition, it very cheap, when compared to the price of a traditional printed book. As explained earlier, ebooks are publishable by using a self-publishers platform. Most of these retailers and distributors are not publishers per se. In fact, you are the publisher of your book and you will assume the responsibility for the quality of work, while the retailers' job is to make your book available on their websites.

You can distinguish a self-publisher from a traditional publisher by comparing the following characteristics:

- It is completely free! Some services never ask you for an upfront fee. Even if you pay some percentage of upfront fees to the hybrid publisher, you will still earn 100% net profit. Some services may ask you to give them a certain percentage of sales proceeds in lieu of sales confirmed by them.
- A self-published author is free to do anything with the book; you can upload your book at any time or withdraw it from the online store if it does not sell well. You can publish new and improved editions, change the cover and graphics to make it more attractive.
- With self-publishing, you do need not be an expert in publishing. You can always use automatic and readily available tools provided by the publisher to design, create and market the book for sale.

Self-publishing services come in different forms and formats. Some of them are retailers, while others are distributors and book builders/ distributors. You can use any one of the following services depending on your needs and requirements:

ebook retailers: A majority of ebook retailers charges some fees in lieu of distributing and selling your ebook through their online storefront. Kindle Direct Publishing is the classic example of an ebook retailer. However, they never help or assist the author in creating the ebook; what they offer is a facility to upload your book in different formats.

ebook distributors: An ebook distributor is an intermediate and sells the book with the help of other retailers and distributors. An author will have the privilege of not dealing with multiple selling channels to sell books. You will just need to deal and interact with only one publishing service. Some of the examples are Smashwords and Pronoun.

Classic book designers, builders, and distributors: An author can create, build, design, format and distribute books through one, solitary platform. If you have a coffee table book, children's fiction or pictorial manuals, then you can use this service, so that you will avoid the hassles of selling the book through multiple channels.

How to create an ebook file for publishing

An appropriately formatted and up-loadable ebook is the first requirement for self-publishing. In fact, a self-publisher will insist on a file that is appropriate for a specific platform for publishing. Some publishers accept only PDF files, while others demand that you upload files in .epub and Mobi formats. Hence, you may have to convert and format your book in different formats many times over in order to upload on different web platforms. Designing, creating, editing and formatting ebook is up to you and you can create your book with your individual effort or you can outsource the entire work to a professional or a freelancer.

The most common formats used to create an ebook are:

EPUB: This is a widely accepted format for ebook publication. Almost all self-publisher accept this format and allow authors to upload their files. You can use special converting software to convert MS Word files to this format.

PDF: It is a difficult format for beginners, because of its difficulty to convert into other popular formats. PDF conversion is time-consuming and you will need to be very careful of formatting errors.

MOBI: You can upload MOBI formats easily on the Amazon Kindle platform. It is also quite convenient to convert your MS Word file into the MOBI format. MOBI is also widely accepted by many self-publishers.

Note: ebook formatting and conversion are two different terms. You will need to be very careful while applying these techniques to your book creation. It is easy to convert files from one format to the other. However, the process of conversion is automated and you will not change editing or styling of the book. The resulting product may actually look very bad and unprofessional if you do not format the book properly. See that you are formatting your book in a professional manner before converting it. The most popular book conversion software systems are Calibre, Kindle Auto Ebook Converter, Epubor, Ultimate Ebook Converter, Zamzar, Hamster Free Ebook Converter, Epubsoft Ebook Converter, and Vellum.

If you feel that the formatting and conversion process is too bothersome to you, then you can hire professional services by paying a conversion fee. If you are publishing a book that is full of pictures, photos, illustrations, tables, and graphics, then you can consider ebook Partnership. On the contrary, if your book contains a lot of text, then you can choose other service providers like Draft2Digital and

Smashwords. Publishing ebooks in children's fiction genre could be difficult because the market is very poor for these books. Likewise, coffee table books with heavy graphics and photographs are difficult to produce, unlike printed ones. It is very tedious to reproduce the color and tone of photographs in an ebook format.

Travel ebooks with vibrant pictures need special treatment to correct reproduction anomalies and errors. Textual ebooks in the popular genre are more likely to do well, as they are simple to convert without any formatting errors. If you want to outsource editing, proofreading, book cover and formatting work to a freelancer, you will have to ask the worker to sign an NDA (Non-Disclosure Agreement) to safeguard your rights. Some of the websites that offer you freelancing services are Freelancer, Upwork, PeopleperHour, Craigslist, Guru, Fiverr, 99Designs and LinkedIn ProFinder. Most of the freelancers who work for these sites are affordable with a budget that does not cut a deep hole in your pocket.

Creating front and back cover are a tricky job. Whatever the image and text you create, it should represent the main concept of the book and its content. All colorized covers (front and back) designed should be vibrant, catchy, not too gaudy, aesthetically pleasing and neatly laid out. Again, cover layout and graphics should be selected very carefully, because plagiarized images could result in copyright notices issued to you. The above-mentioned freelancing sites provide a big list of freelancers who can work at comparatively cheaper rates.

Finding a suitable self-publisher

Once your book is ready, you will need to find a very good self-publishing service that can take care of your needs and requirements. Here are some the well-known self-publishing sites:

CreateSpace

One of the trustworthy, self-publisher, CreateSpace has a great distribution service called *Expanded Distribution* that provides you an opportunity to get into a bigger market consisting of online retailers, bookstores, institutions, and distributors within the United States and elsewhere in the world. Every author will need to make his or her books discoverable by many people and CreateSpace ensures you this facility. A subsidiary of Amazon, CreateSpace is one of the leading media development and book publishing firms that cater to the varied demands of thousands of authors. One of the significant advantages of using this channel is the readily available Amazon market.

You can sell your book to both public and private readership audience, while the site allows you to upload books only in PDF format. Amazon's proprietary Kindle-style is the allowed system for download. It is easy to get an ISBN number for your book too. Although CreateSpace allows you to design and create soft cover titles, hardcover books cannot be created at present. Message boards and forum participation could be messy at times because of the absence of social media tools that can extend the social reach. With CreateSpace, you can easily reach faraway markets in Europe and Great Britain.

CreateSpace' average pricing package to create books is quite reasonable. A standard B&W title starts at $3.66 and the maximum price is pegged at $39 that comes under Pro Plan that allows you keep more from each sale. You can use a standard royalty chart to find out the cost of the book and royalty based on the number of pages and book interior type and trim size. The chart displayed below gives you an example of calculating royalty: Let us assume that you want to create a book (250 pages) in black and white color with a trim size measurement of 5.5" by 8.5". You can calculate both the list price and royalty amount by using the chart. Here, you can make $2.15 on the Amazon home portal, $4.15 through the store and $0.15 by the way of expanded distribution.

For different print options, interior types, length of the book in pages and trim size, you can calculate the royalty accrued in terms of money. Obviously, the royalty payment seems to the best when you choose to sell your book through the CreateSpace store. CreateSpace seems to offer a better alternative for authors to earn far lucrative royalty rates when compared to the one that is offered by other self-publishing websites. In spite of its popularity among self-publishing authors, CreateSpace remains a front for Amazon to generate its corporate profits. Nevertheless, it is a very beneficial tool for aspiring authors to earn some decent income through self-generated books.

Royalty Calculator *
Use the royalty calculator to figure out how much you'll make every time your book is manufactured.

Interior Type	Black and White		Number of Pages	250
Trim Size	5.5" x 8.5"			

			Amazon.com	$2.15
USD $	10.00	Calculate	eStore	$4.15
			Expanded Distribution	$0.15

☑ Yes, suggest GBP price based on the U.S. price

			Amazon Europe	
GBP £	7.58	Calculate	For books printed in Great Britain	£1.34

☑ Yes, suggest EUR price based on the U.S. price

			Amazon Europe	
EUR €	8.34	Calculate	For books printed in continental Europe	€1.40

* Figures generated by this tool are for estimation purposes only. Your actual royalty will be calculated when you set up your book.

When you pay for a specific package, you get customized front and back cover design, ISBN services, local and global distribution, 24x7 author support, book interior design and layout and image insertion after editing. Another advantage is your ability to publish books in other popular formats like Nook, iPad, iPhone, Android, and Kobo. Author discounts and free copies are also included in the package. Front and back cover design includes pre-made templates, cover support, and different themes. All these services are included in the basic package. If you want to choose a graphic artist for your book, you will need to choose premium service at a slightly higher price. You can consult one of the professionals to discuss the package of your choice and seek practical suggestions about the procedure that goes beyond publishing a book.

Amazon Kindle

By far, Amazon Kindle is the most famous and well-recognized self-publication service in the world. Kindle's audience is massive and its reach is spread far and across the world. Amazon Kindle provides you an access to readers living in all major countries in the world. The downside with Kindle is the perceived limitations related to designing and formatting ebooks, especially when the book contents are varied and diverse.

Amazon offers two modes of publishing: Kindle Direct Publishing and KDP Select. Both of these formats will help you set up connections with thousands of online readers and prospective buyers. If you price your ebook between $2.99 and $9.99, the royalty paid out will be 70%. KDP version requires you that you sell your book only on Amazon and nowhere else. KDP Select is by far the best choice for you because it allows you to distribute your book free for five days or it also grants discounts to readers for up to seven days through an offer called Countdown Deal; your share of royalty during this discount offer schedule is still 70%. In the meanwhile, you will earn just 35% of royalties, if you charge book below $2.99. If you are subscribing to KDP program, you can include your book in Kindle Owner's Lending Library, which is free of cost to Prime members. This option may not bring you huge sales, but it is still a useful tool to spread awareness about the book and its content. If you have more than two or three books in your name, you can easily sign up for Countdown Deals, because they can draw readers' attention to other titles.

.MOBI is the book format that is specific to the Kindle, although you upload your book in different other types like Doc, RTF, and ePub. Conversion could be a time-consuming process with Kindle. Make sure that you do test conversions at least 10 times before finalizing the book. Conversion is quicker, while conversion quality standard is set to very high. On the day of the launch, make sure that your book is ready in every aspect; conversion should be properly carried out with clear formatting, good font setting, properly aligned images, perfect cover art, graphics, and appropriate back cover with a brief synopsis of the book. Uploading is quite simple too with a quick uploading speed. You can select the most appropriate section to upload because keywords should match the content of the book; otherwise, readers may not find your book when they search for titles. You can give your loyal readers something to remember; it could be a free review copy or even a very low buying price of $0.99.

Charging your Kindle book involves several parameters and you may wish to consider them in order to set the most appropriate price. Some of these parameters are as follows:

- The rate of royalty per sale
- The pricing structure of other books that compare to your book
- Content and its quality
- Book-length in terms of word count
- Size of upload

- Book genre and classification
- Geographic locality
- Total review and sample copies given out before the book launch

Amazon offers its Kindle subscribers two basic price structures: if you price your book between $0.99 and $9.99, the royalty payout is 70% of the cover price. Anything beyond these suggested prices will get you just 35% royalty. Most authors choose a pricing point for their book at cheaper rates of $0.99, $4.99 and $9.99 and receive a royalty rate of 70% in the process. Some authors sell their books at a very low price of $0.99 (99 cents) because many external sites advertise low priced Kindle books on their sites. If you sell more numbers, you can enhance your Amazon author sales rank too. It is also possible to invite a large number of people to review your book when you break a threshold point of sales.

Usually, authors set a selling price based on the length of the book, in terms of word counts or pages. For example, you can charge 99 cents for a book with 10 pages (up to 5000 words) content, $1.99 for a title with 20 pages (5000-10000 words) content and $2.99 for a book with 30 pages (10000-30000 words) content. The overall average price per book works out to 10 – 12 cents per page. The best selling price for an Amazon Kindle book is $2.99.

iBooks, NOOK, and Kobo

Apple's iBooks is one of the premier ebook centers for reading on iPad, iPhone and iTouch devices. One can easily purchase books by using iBooks application that is available as a free download through iTunes. Similarly, Barnes and Noble's NOOK also help readers buy and read ebooks through its global websites. Two of the visible advantages of using NOOK format is the availability of the book for download throughout the world and better marketability of the book that is ensured by global online bookstores. Kobo ebook store is yet another destination for self-publication. Kobo is one of the largest ebook distributors in the world and it controls 25% of the global ebook market. The royalty offered by these publishers is as attractive and cajoling as offers made by any other publisher in the world.

Self-publishing offers you a myriad of choices and options. Apart from the publishers mentioned elsewhere in the book, you can also try out others like Gardner's Books, Baker and Taylor, eCentral, Scribd, Ciando, EBSCO, Vearsa, BLURB, CafePress, Webook, and Xlibris. In the meanwhile, you may also like to check out their royalty offers and book rights before signing a self-publishing contract.

Is self-publishing profitable at all?

Self-publishing is profitable as long as you find a publisher, who can give you maximum profit possible. For example, you choose a service that lets you keep 100% of the profit. Similarly, you can also consider picking up a publisher, who takes a small cut of your overall sales; these publishers help you with profit sharing and in the form of the book distribution by collaborating with other online retailers. Sell publishing is a difficult career option. Making money from self-publishing requires utmost patience, attention, dedication, common sense and hard work. The extent of success that you can expect from self-publishing depends on various factors like the content of your book, self-publication outlet, presentation of book, market and promotion plan, social media outreach and income sharing plan offered by the publisher. The following table gives you a thematic analysis of income that you can generate by selling ebooks in some of the most popular channels like Amazon, Nook Press, Apple iBooks and Kobo.

ebook Retailer	ebook Price - 99 cent	ebook Price - $2.99	ebook Price - $9.99
Amazon	33 cents (35%)	$2.09 (70%)	$6.99 (70%)
Nook Press	40 cents (40%)	$1.94 (65%)	$6.49 (65%)
Apple iBooks	70 cents (70%)	$2.09 (70%)	$6.99 (70%)
Kobo	45 cents (45%)	$2.09 (70%)	$6.99 (70%)

Selling ebook on Amazon, Nook, iBooks, and Kobo is quite profitable. Choose a self-publishing service that helps you sell your book through these bookstores because you can maximize your income-earning plan at no extra cost. You can self-publish and make a print edition available for sale through a POD (print on demand) service. POD helps you sell printed books one at a time whenever a customer orders for them. With POD, you can reduce your financial risk, because you are not asking your publisher to print multiple copies at the same time. There is very little upfront cost involved, while the printed books are available for order in all the major outlets like Amazon, Powell's, Barnes and

Noble, Alibris and others. A POD book looks almost similar to a traditional printed book, at least for printed black and white books. However, the unit cost of a POD printed book is on the higher side.

Earning and maximizing profits should be your ultimate goal. You can use Ingram Spark and CreateSpace if you want to publish POD printed books and sell them on an order-by-order basis. You can also sell Ingram Spark on all selling channels except the Amazon. Likewise, CreateSpace allows you to sell printed books during Amazon Sales events. Financially, publishing printed books through Amazon is much more profitable, because most bookstores rarely order books provided by CreateSpace through Amazon. It just takes two days to publish a printed book on Amazon, while you need more than two weeks to see your book on Ingram Spark online bookshelves. The following illustration illuminates more about POD earning:

For a $14.99, standard, 6x9 paperback (250-275 pages content):

	Ingram Spark	CreateSpace
Printing cost per book	$3.94	$3.63
Earning, when sold on Amazon	$2.41	$5.36
Earning, when sold outside of Amazon	$2.41	$2.36

Optimizing profits with your self-publishing business is possible only when you explore available publishing channels other than Kindle; even with Kindle's popularity, you can still choose a good publisher that pays decent royalties. A mixture of Nook, Kobo, iBooks, Ingram Spark and CreateSpace along with Kindle is a potentially money-making combination that drives a good amount of profits. Many authors make the mistake of choosing a print run for their book. In fact, it could be a foolish decision in the end as you will be selling a ton of books. The minimum copies that a publisher wants you to order is 1000 copies. Sometimes this seems almost impossible and very expensive. This is a dangerous decision when you publish both printed and ecopies of the same book simultaneously. Print on demand or POD could be a practical decision because you only pay for what you sell to your customers. In other words, POD would be a wise and smart business solution, if you mix it with ebook publication.

Self-publishing is a beautiful concept! It permits you to retain all rights with you. However, some over-zealous self-publishers may ask for a share of book rights. Ceding even smaller fraction rights could create a future dent in your pocket because you stand to lose money in the process. For example, giving away movie script rights and audio rights could lead to financial losses in the future. Some publishers may even ask for a "right of first refusal" for any succeeding books that you publish with them. A publisher is responsible for income loss in the domain of self-publishing by charging excessive upfront fees. Most of these costs belong to ballooning "back-end" costs charged sometime during the process of creation of the book.

One area where the publisher may charge you hidden upfront fees is in author copy purchases; author copies may be twice as expensive as the copies you could order if you are self-publishing. Self-publishing is a self-driven entrepreneurial venture when you will be investing money to publish a book and hope to earn money by selling maximum numbers of books possible. Normally speaking, the overall business you make with your book, should be at least five times more than the expenditure involved in bringing the book to the store. Lowly priced ebooks are the best bet if you want to self-publish. These books are cheaper to produce, easy to upload and bring to the stores and cost-effective for the buyer. Furthermore, a virtual book is made exclusively for reading devices that can be carried anywhere and at any time.

While calculating the royalty amount, you should also know the difference between net and gross royalty. Take a classic example of POD printed book (let us leave out ebook because we already know the royalty percentage offered by major retailers). The numbers can vary because of the complex calculation involved.

Let us also assume that your royalty is 40 percent of the retail price less printing cost. Here is the calculation:

Selling price of the book: $15.00

Cost of printing each book: $ 6.00

Royalty payable to you: $15 - $6 = $9 x 40 percent = $3.60/book

Some of the hidden costs charged by the publisher:

Credit card for each transaction: up to 4%

Higher cost production of each book: at least over $4 per book that was actually charged $15 to the author.

More often, publisher charge an inflated cost to print each book and royalty payout will be on this net inflated price. In many cases, the publisher will work the cost flow in the following manner:

Net royalty calculation - Printing markup cost as a fraction of the cost of printing each book. In most of the cases, the publisher will usually mask this figure.

Here is a numerical example:

Let us assume that you are printing a 250 page, 6 inches by 9 inches paperback fiction. Let us also presume that it costs $4.00 to print the book (including $0.014 per page and $0.50 per cover). Let us also believe that this book sells for $15.90. In most of the cases, a royalty is calculated based on the policies designed by individual websites. Let us take it as 50%. If you evaluate the actual print cost in finding out the royalty amount, you can highlight this scenario:

Retail price: $15.90 - Less - Actual printing cost: $4.00

Profit split equally between the author and publisher: $11.90

Author royalty: $5.95

However, if the publisher decides to fix the printing cost at $5.00, what happens next?

> *Retail price: $15.90*
>
> *Inflated and increased printing cost: $ 5.00*
>
> *Less*
>
> *The amount comes to $10.90*

Splitting this amount equally between the author and publisher (50% royalty), the amount comes to $5.45. Obviously, the royalty amount is lesser than the actual one. Here, the publisher also makes the same money plus markup cost of extra $1.00 that equals to $6.45! This is what experts on self-publishing call: "the double rinse!" Here, the publisher will make money on each sale and from both ends. In other words, many publishers consider and define "net price based on their whims and fancies!" A similar situation may also occur when a publisher offers trade-discount to authors to purchase books for personal use and distribution to friends and acquaintances.

Tip: Never deal with a publisher who charges trade-discounts, administrative and managerial costs and marketing/promotional costs. These costs can actually bring down the royalty amount that eventually results in enormous overheads and potential losses.

Master checklist for calculating royalties:

- Find out whether the calculation is based on retail price or the net sales figure. You may wish to talk to the publisher about net sales amount

- Valuate actual cost of production vs. inflated printing cost. Bargain for a better cost per book
- Ask, if the publisher needs a higher minimum retail cost to print books. You can provide a price comparison list by including charges and costs provided by other publishers in the industry
- Find out the quantum of royalty payable to the author. Never ever, consider a royalty amount lesser than 50%. Rather, insist on at least 60% payment.

10. FINAL WORDS ON SELF-PUBLISHING

As mentioned before, self-publishing your book can be lucrative and profitable. However, things may look too challenging for first-time authors. It might look discouraging for you to read some of the the things we talked about in this book. However, the overall exercise of publishing a book is quite exciting and truly rewarding. We are sure that you are serious about publishing your book. You may be even be trying to talk to other self-publishers. We hope you understand that there are many people willing to help you in this process. Whether you hire a hybrid publisher or pitch your book to a literary agent and forgo the traditional publishing route, we wish you success. We would like to remind you that you are a racehorse in a tightly packed race full of many racehorses. We are confident that if you persist and continue to the end, you will be the winning horse at the finish line.

The views expressed here are exhausting and they provide a multi-dimensional view of the traditional and self-publishing world. We are sure that you will start running and get to the finish line faster than ever. To succeed as a self-published author, you will need to be creative and success hungry. We hope that the practical tips provided in this book are easy to understand and comprehend. We also know that you have an amazing book inside of your head. You will just need an outlet to let that book come out to the public. Self-publishing could be the best platform for you to allow that bestselling book out. Go ahead and taste success.

Good luck on your success! Get your book published and have a great writing day!

ABOUT THE AUTHORS

Jenn Foster is one of today's national leading online and mobile marketing experts, an award winning web designer, author and sought after speaker and trainer. Jenn is the owner of Elite Online Publishing and the founder and CEO of Biz Social Boom, companies dedicated to helping business owners of all sizes thrive in today's highly technical world of product and service promotion. She is a ten-time bestselling author. She is passionate about helping busy entrepreneurs, business leaders, and professional athletes create, publish, and market their book, to build their business and brand. She encourages new authors to share their stories, knowledge and expertise to help others. Jenn Foster has an entrepreneur family background, her grandfather started the Maverik Country Stores convenience store chain and oil/fuel distribution dynasty currently operating in the Western United States. Jenn has over 15 years of retail business experience online and offline. Jenn enjoys spending time with her three children, experiencing the great outdoors and she loves playing music on her viola and piano. amazon.com/author/jennfoster

Melanie Churella Johnson is a ten-time bestselling author. She is a speaker, coach, and consultant. Melanie was honored to be a TEDx speaker in Sugarland, Texas in 2016 where she spoke on the importance of leaving a legacy: "Leaving a Legacy - The Time is Now". She has owned and operated two independent TV stations in Houston and Dallas. She has been in front of and behind the camera. Melanie started her career as a News Anchor in Detroit at Channel 20 after she won the title of Miss Michigan and was the first runner up to Miss America. She is currently the owner of Elite Online Publishing and Charity Auction Consignments. She is passionate about sharing people's stories that, educate, motivate and inspire. She is an expert at publishing, marketing and positioning nonfiction books for business owners and professionals. She creates expert authority status for marketing impact and influence. She is honored to work one on one with her authors to create the best strategies for book creation, marketing, and social media. She is the host of two podcasts on iTunes and Stitcher Radio. "Hot Chicks Write Hot Books" and "Elite Expert Insider". Melanie has two teenage boys and resides in Houston Texas. She loves spending time with her family, shopping and traveling. amazon.com/author/melaniejohnson

To get help publishing or marketing your book visit

EliteOnlinePublishing.com

There you can find current publishing and marketing tools, tips and secrets.

www.ingramcontent.com/pod-product-compliance
Lightning Source LLC
Chambersburg PA
CBHW071006120626
46546CB00003B/961